Jack Teagarden

The Story of a Jazz Maverick

Jack Teagarden

The Story of a Jazz Maverick

by
Jay D. Smith
and
Len Guttridge

New Preface by Martin Williams

A DA CAPO PAPERBACK

Library of Congress Cataloging in Publication Data

Smith, Jay D.
  Jack Teagarden: the story of a jazz maverick / Jay D. Smith and Len Gut-
tridge.
    (A Da Capo paperback)
    Reprint. Originally published: London: Cassell, 1960. With new pref.
    ISBN 0-306-80322-4
    1. Teagarden Jack, 1905-1964. 2. Jazz musicians — United States — Biography.
I. Guttridge, Leonard F. II. Title.
ML419.T25S6   1988
788'.2'0924 — dc19   87-34670

Published by Da Capo Press, Inc.
A Subsidiary of Plenum Publishing Corporation
233 Spring Street, New York, N.Y. 10013

Preface to the Da Capo Edition

In 1950, on the occasion of his 50th birthday, Louis Armstrong granted a long and generally fascinating interview to the editors of a magazine called the *Record Changer*. The publication was read by jazz record collectors, so there were many questions about Armstrong's early days and about his musical relationship to his mentor Joseph "King" Oliver. It was the elder cornetist who first brought the young Armstrong out of New Orleans, and who was an early influence on his style. Louis, as usual, was properly respectful of "Papa Joe." But he made it clear that he also wanted to talk about his current "brass team," and about Jack Teagarden. He rated that later musical relationship most highly, higher than any such he had ever known, it is safe to say.

The meshing of Armstrong and Teagarden was a close one musically, no question. And it was partly a matter of Louis's own sizable effect on everybody's music. However much he was inspired by Oliver, Armstrong has offered music something new, something which Oliver, for all his accomplishments and importance, had merely hinted at — a new rhythmic sense, a new momentum, a *swing* based on several things, even on a new way of sounding the individual notes. Jack Teagarden was one of the first trombonists to absorb that Armstrong sense of swing in the Armstrong manner.

Teagarden's musical personality and demeanor were distinctly and unmistakably his own, however. Indeed, what Louis contributed could inspire the singularly concentrated ease of a Jack Teagarden on the one band, and (let us say) the stark three-minute dramas of a Billie Holiday on the other. And it could allow each of those artists (and hundreds of others) also to be themselves.

As I say, Teagarden was himself. And he was, technically speaking, a superb trombonist, a superb brassman. In the late

i

1950s, composer-arranger Bill Russo, himself a trombonist, declared that he had decided that Teagarden was, after all, *the* best trombone-player — and this at a time when a J.J. Johnson-inspired bebop virtuosity reigned supreme on the instrument, especially among the young. Earlier, Teagarden's 1950 recording of his dazzling variations on Richard Rodgers's *Lover* (a Broadway waltz converted into an up-tempo 4/4) was admired by young and old alike. And by audiences as well, for *Lover* quickly became something of a set-piece for Jack, joining *Stars Fell on Alabama, Basin Street Blues, St. James Infirmary* and *I Gotta Right to Sing the Blues* as a standard part of his almost-nightly repertory.

Most of the Teagarden standards were slower than *Lover,* of course, and they partly depended on the singular character of what has been called "the Teagarden aura." However, in those slower vehicles Jack's techniques often showed themselves at their best. His was an art of flourishes and ornaments, but flourishes so discreetly conceived and placed as to enhance and never draw attention to themselves. And his ornaments were executed with perfectly controlled combinations of the right embouchure and slide co-ordination. Perhaps only Ellington's virtuoso trombonist Lawrence Brown could rival them. And they depended on such quick, flexible lip techniques that perhaps only a man like trumpeter Harry Edison, some years later, might have challenged them.

The "live" recordings made at the remarkable 1947 Louis Armstrong All Stars, and of which you'll read more in these pages, were later issued on LP, and they show Jack's art succinctly. Here was Teagarden, mind you, on stage with Armstrong, and Armstrong was the kind of performer who needed only to walk in front of an audience to gain its full attention. And who needed only to blow a few of his powerful, authoritative notes to confirm that attention. In Teagarden's half-chorus solo on *Pennies from Heaven* (an Armstrong vehicle, after all) Jack distilled that piece's melody line to a simple, all-but-original lyric statement, and then ornamented his own lovely phrases with superbly understated terminal flourishes. And of course he made it all sound paradoxically easy. Then Jack, at center stage, played and sang *St. James Infirmary* with such totally straightforward, cool concentration that one would be hard put not to hang on to his every note and phrase.

Talk about a Teagarden aura! As if to say, "There is Louis's power (God bless him) and here is mine, and you see they aren't the same."

Obviously a man like Teagarden, with his mastery of his instrument, might have stepped into almost any kind of music and made a career for himself. But one thing that Jay D. Smith's and Len Guttridge's book makes clear is that Jack could not have been any kind of musician except a jazz musician. A jazz musician simply has to make his music and dedicate his life to it, even though he may not tell you (or himself) *why* he has to. He may not, indeed, even be able to say why, or need to say why. The need is to make the music and, necessarily, lead the life that makes that possible. All of which has little or nothing to do with ego or acclaim or money. He needs to give his music to the world and he hopes the world will understand.

You will find out about that need in these pages. You will also find plenty of the pranks and boys-will-be-boys anecdotes that seem so prevalent, diverting, and (under the surface) necessary a part of the musical life.

I could say that Smith and Guttridge engaged in a labor of love in researching and writing their book for Jack. But I would also describe it as a labor of infatuation, and I offer that further description with respect.

— Martin Williams
October 1987

List of Illustrations

Foreword

It is rather frustrating to be asked to write the foreword to one's own biography. What else can be said when your life is unfolded like a map with the roads you travelled now dim trails.

Sometimes I ask myself if the journey was worth it. Especially at those times when I've regretted the day I first picked up the trombone (when I was barely old enough to lift it). During the winter of 1958-9 I was on a global road tour and too busy to ask myself any questions other than those dealing with transport and accommodation.

That these were efficiently dealt with is mainly due to Addie whose devotion and good humour have survived many a strain. Believe me, if there's one more demanding job for a woman than being married to a working jazz musician, it's acting as his band manager. Addie does both admirably.

Yes, after that round-the-world jaunt through better than a dozen countries, entertaining multitudes of Indians, Afghans, Pakistanis, Ceylonese, Burmese, Malays, Thais, Cambodians, Laotians, Japanese, Koreans, Formosans, Philippinos, Okinawans and Chinese. I've not much doubt that my forty-year jazz record was worth the price I've sometimes paid to make it. It was worth it that November night in Rangoon when the President of Burma pinned Tenderfoot badges on the bandsmen and myself while all the boy scouts in Burma cheered. Worth it to know that I could consider the royal families of Cambodia and Thailand as truly personal friends. Worth it to hear the applause of fifty thousand Chinese soldiers echo across the Formosan hills and to know with an indefinable emotion that although I had played *Basin Street* countless times it had never been heard in a stranger setting. Sure, I heard plenty of speeches about how musicians travelling abroad helped to strengthen friendship between nations, and of course they are very true. But far more eloquent than the greetings of a Minister of Culture or the praise of a Prime Minister were the smiles, cheers and handshakes of the people of Kabul, Pnompenh and Ipoh, places I had never heard of, whose names I still can't pronounce, but which are to the folk who live there more important than London and Paris and New York.

There aren't many of us old-timers left, the ones the writers call *mainstreamers*. But believe me, none of us could ask a greater reward from jazz than I found. Fats, Bunny, the Dorseys and Art Tatum are gone, and I wonder if any of the youngsters can ever take their places. It's hard to find a kid nowadays who has a spark of built-in talent and wants to learn jazz the only way it can be learned—by sacrifice and hard knocks. Today's proving ground is the recording studio rather than the speakeasy and the big band. If one shows talent he can get a job with any of a thousand trios or quartets and chances are he'll become a star overnight—recording nowadays is too easy. And unless he approaches music in humility, he'll be an old man of jazz by his mid-twenties, burned out because he has nothing fresh to say. If music truly comes from the heart, it seems to me that there should always be *something* new to say.

The acceptance of jazz abroad was the greatest thing that ever happened to it. Everyone associated with it should feel proud. Why, I remember when polite folks looked down their noses at it even right in America. Thank heaven they don't any more, and the chief trouble now comes from people who seem to think that everything a man blows must have a label pinned on it as if it were a dead bug in a box instead of a very live thing. Even today some people ask me what style I play. Others don't even bother to ask—they *tell* me. But I don't know, I never tagged the way I blow and I don't know of any real jazz musician who does. Good or bad, it's jazz—that's all. Many forces and circumstances shape the manner in which a man creates and they differ in each case. I don't know whether this book will help explain why I play the way I do. Maybe it doesn't matter much anyway. But this is the story of my life in jazz. It's all here from intro to coda.

Prelude

IT was December in Pittsburgh and long after midnight. Along Brownsville Road all the clubs but one were dark. The Bali Kea still glowed and commotion stirred on its steps. A bus drew up bearing the words DORSEY BROTHERS and unloaded musicians and instruments.

Inside, the mock Hawaiian murals faced on to empty tables. The last customers had gone home but the stale scents of whiskey and tobacco lingered. On the stand, the club's band of the week was winding up another night. Instruments were being dismantled, cleaned, packed away. The men worked unhurriedly, took their time over the last cigarette, exchanged typical tired after-hours' banter.

They were not young men. Their leader was erect, broad-shouldered and fifty with a smile half that age. A slow lazy smile, touched with sadness. That's how it had always been. Ever since he changed his name from Weldon to Jack Teagarden.

He looked up in disbelief as the entire orchestra of Jimmy and Tommy Dorsey pushed its way into the club. It was followed by a second line of local musicians and selected guests. And from then till dawn a tribute was paid. Not a formal tribute, nobody presented anything, nobody made any speeches—coherent ones, anyway. Emotion was there but expressed only in handshakes and backslaps. And in music.

The Dorseys represented many years of commercial dance-band success. In this year of 1955 they were still before the public eye on television. And from the hotel where they were currently featured the brothers had brought their whole band to greet a friend and fellow musician who was nowhere near the top. Commercially, that is. Of course, terms like success and failure are meaningless. Long ago Jack reached this conclusion after having frequent difficulty telling the two apart.

He was no retired has-been. His name might have little impact on the new generation of faddists. But their idols, the modern jazz masters of the nineteen-fifties, know they are merely building on foundations laid by Teagarden and his associates. If what they build is often frail and hollow, the fault is not in the foundation.

So he was one of the great architects of jazz. Both the white and Negro races have produced them. Many are gone and forgotten. Some yielded to ephemeral trends—and are forgotten. A few rose to fame and hung on even if to do so meant jettisoning artistic principles. Jack deserted no principles and won no lasting prosperity. A grand trombonist and the finest white jazz singer of them all, he was a most irresponsible man. At fifty, his total riches amounted to little more than the affection of surviving contemporaries, the respect of the younger musicians and the devotion of jazz lovers the world over.

This means everything or nothing, depending upon your point of view.

The Bali Kea meeting was a salute to Teagarden. It was, too, a reunion. Reunions beget memories.

The Dorseys' men mingled with Teagarden's smaller unit and black coffee was piped in from the kitchen. Buddy Rich joined Ray Bauduc at the drums. Jimmy with his saxophone and Tommy with his trombone stood alongside Jack. They talked old times and played their horns, then talked some more until music and remembrance merged and each jazz chorus was a flight of memory.

And Jack sang. His voice, someone has said, is musical even in speech, strong-fibred and rich in song. He sings like an angel, but an angel from Texas, gone a little maverick. . . .

I went down to St. James Infirmary . . . Off with the bell, on with the water glass and look out there, here's the oldest blues I ever heard. But was there ever a time when he didn't hear the blues inside him?

Basin Street is the street where . . . Where he hunted a clarinet player for Peck after Rapollo left and he heard that cornet flare

over the river and he ran down Canal Street to meet Louis
alighting from the boat, all gleams and guffaws. . . .

I'd rather drink muddy water, Lord . . . And those Chicago
boys were sometimes doing just that. Living from hand to
mouth, said Eddie Condon, and usually it was somebody else's
hand. . . .

Love, oh love, oh loveless love . . . She told him, Jack, you love
music, gin and me—in that order. Who told him? Was it Ora?
Clare? Billie? No matter, now. . . .

I've got a right to sing the blues . . . His dreams were ashes at
his feet then and although the world around him was crying
the blues they weren't his kind of blues and he was utterly
lonely. . . .

I was born at midnight, by morning I could talk . . . In a sense
life did begin for him one Christmas eve at midnight although
he was eight years old by then. Who lives until he has first
tasted disappointment. . . ?

The year was 1913. . . .

Chapter I

. . . THE town was Vernon, a one-time cattle station up near the Texas Panhandle. Two young parents were carefully trimming a Christmas tree. Or, to be more accurate, the household coat rack. They couldn't afford a real tree.

The couple worked in silence, to avoid disturbing the two children asleep in the next room. When the younger one, an infant girl, woke up crying, the mother sighed and hastened to her. Her son was also awake but soundless and staring at the ceiling. As soon as the girl was restored to sleep the mother made to leave. His voice checked her.

'Mom,' he said softly, 'don't forget to turn the damper down on the stove.'

'Why?'

'If Santa sees the light he'll think we're still up. And he won't stop at our house.'

She crossed to the boy, kissed him and returned to the 'tree'. She was placing a crudely wrapped package beneath it when a sound disturbed her. She turned. The boy was standing in the doorway watching them. The scene before him annihilated his every dream of a visiting, gift-laden Santa. He felt confused and betrayed.

For a moment the grown-ups were uncertain. Then the mother took his hand and led him to the tree. She showed him his gift. And though tears of disillusionment continued to scald his eyes, Jack Teagarden, at eight, smiled quiveringly upon his first trombone.

It was by no means his first meeting with music. Already he had rescued a rusting tenor-valve horn from the oblivion of a corner closet and had mastered it sufficiently to accompany his mother, a confident pianist, and his father, a less confident cornettist, at family musicales. He was not so much a first-born son as he was the tiniest member of a dedicated trio of musicians.

A paucity of space in the Teagarden home made practice difficult. The musical urges of each demanded more elbow room. Friction resulted and the instrumental sound which issued from the house at the bottom of Mesquite Street was not always harmonious. But there were many evenings when personal strivings were subordinated to the group, when family unity was purely expressed in music. When love for each other joined pride in their playing to touch the melody with rare sweetness. Such moments reminded Helen and Charles Teagarden of their courtship.

Helen was one of five daughters born to an immigrant named Henry Geingar who had exchanged the iron militarism of Bismarck for more placid environments in Pennsylvania. He married Tillie Foulk, a Dutch girl, and they moved to Electra, Texas. When Helen was born Henry was working as section foreman for the Fort Worth & Denver Railroad. His wife meanwhile ran a small hotel.

The fantastic era of the great cattle drives was drawing to a close. Near-by Vernon was the last supply base on the Western Trail before a desolate three-hundred-mile journey to the busy Kansas rail heads. Here, just south of the Red River, the chuckwagons were loaded, trail masters outfitted with saddles, ropes, ammunition. Here, fresh horses were bought, equipment repaired and cowboy thirsts slaked before the bellowing mass of cattle was pointed northwards to the river and the wild country beyond. The vast mesquite and buffalo grass plains of north and west Texas were the domain of the cattle barons. They lived luxuriously in ranch palaces and upon their fabulous wealth was founded the lasting, if less spectacular, prosperity of settlements like Vernon and Electra. Indeed, Electra was named for the daughter of W. T. Waggoner, one of the mightiest of the millionaire ranch lords.

Like other big Texas railroads the F. W. and D. was pushing ever westward; and while Henry Geingar contributed to its expansion his wife devoted herself to the challenging tasks of rearing six children and administering to a hotel clientele consisting chiefly of uninhibited ranch hands and sophisticated salesmen. As five of the children were girls, the situation was not without its hazards. Tillie Geingar may be forgiven if she displayed some haste in marrying her daughters off at an early age. She did not overlook their cultural training though, and employed the services of a handsome German named Paul Goetze who came fifteen miles from Iowa Park once a week to teach the piano. Soon, whenever a guest at the hotel ventured into song, he would receive prompt accompaniment from any one of the Geingar girls at the hardy old upright in the lobby.

Business was good, the Geingars themselves owned a considerable acreage and young Guy Waggoner paid court to Helen with his father's approval. Furthermore, the Geingar hotel, though eminently respectable, still had its quota of young bloods on the register. Clearly, it was no place for a growing girl. So circumstances seemed to support the Waggoner boy's proposal of marriage. But Tillie Geingar considered other attributes than wealth to be at least equally precious in a prospective son-in-law. Her Dutch shrewdness had already detected an abundance of these traits in the character of young Charlie Teagarden.

The Teagardens were truly of Texas stock. Among the pioneers who first invaded the hostile realm of buffalo and Comanche there had been Teagardens. They survived the Indian raids only to split during the Civil War. The schism was so distinct that a Teagarden who switched his allegiance to the Northern cause changed the spelling to Teegarden. Thus he and his heirs were spared the embarrassment of being confused with their rebel relatives.

The Teagarden outpost at Rondo, seven miles from Electra,

was a large one and quite poor. Only at week-ends was it enriched by the wealth of music and good fellowship. This custom of home musicales was destined to vanish at the spread of radio and the later, fatal assault of the cathode ray screen. But at the turn of the century such homely gatherings formed an essential part of the social structure, especially in rural areas. They fulfilled the twin purpose of emphasizing family bonds and encouraging individual talents. Their passing is no small loss.

When Helen met Charlie she was ten. He was eleven years older and impressed her at first as just another grown-up but somewhat more entertaining than most. Later there were times when the kerosene lamp burned low, someone with a violin and someone else with a harp did gentle things to *Sweetheart Mine* and Helen touched the piano softly and looked at Charlie with a new shyness.

Meanwhile, life at the hotel was less tranquil. For Tillie Geingar proposed selling their land and met with Henry's instant opposition. Their subsequent rift was a by-product of the industrial changes then overtaking the entire Lone Star State. As the demands of the cattlemen grew the supply of watering places dwindled. All over west Texas well-drillers worked feverishly. A contemporary journalist wrote, 'Texas is bringing the water up from below . . . this punching of holes down into the earth has become general. Now, Texas is getting to be like a pin cushion. . . .'

In the locality of Electra the 'pin cushion' was yielding something else. Black and poisonous to cattle, oil's ultimate significance was nowhere fully realized and only suspected by dreamers. Henry Geingar was one. But at his mention of oil Tillie flared. Oil? She had no faith in it. Hadn't W. T. Waggoner, himself seeking water for his huge herds of white-face cattle, stated flatly he didn't want to find oil on his property?

'Hell,' he said, 'ruin all that good grazing land?' So Tillie, satisfied that their property was of no further value as pasture, sold it for a meagre sum. During the transaction Henry was heard to mutter several times something about oil. Nobody paid him much attention.

They moved to Vernon, bought a brick hotel and called it the Panhandle. Soon afterwards, word came from Electra. Oil was gushing all over and the largest wells were on the old Geingar land. W. T. Waggoner studied the black stuff seeping into his precious water, swallowed his prejudices and went on to make even bigger fortunes than his cattle had brought him. The two-million-dollar Arlington Downs race track was for years a lavish symbol of the Waggoner wealth until the state ban on horse racing reduced it to little more than a forlorn landmark.

In 1903 Helen Geingar became Mrs. Charles Teagarden. Fort Worth is less than two hundred miles from Vernon, but to Helen, setting out on her honeymoon, it was as far from home as the moon. She had never left her family before. She was thirteen.

As they approached Fort Worth, Charlie sensed the change in his bride's demeanour. The warm aura of romance which surrounded their departure from Vernon had yielded to a vaguely melancholy mood. When they reached the Grand Hotel the girl tried by forced gaiety to conceal her growing loneliness. But it increased, and was fed by the stronger, more basic, child's fear of marriage. She sat in silence, trembling.

'What is it?' whispered Charlie. He was afraid to touch her lest she flinch. She looked up at him helplessly. Then the meaning of her fears became clear. The hurt softened. Helen was his wife, true, but she was young enough to be, above all, a lonely homesick kid.

'Wait,' he said and left her. He wasn't gone very long. When he returned, his face wore an almost boyish expression of self-assurance.

'There's a music store down the street.' Gently he placed his purchase before her. 'I bought this for you.' It was a bright new mandolin. She gazed at it for some moments. Gradually the cloud lifted. Then she smiled at her husband, picked up the instrument and began to play.

When they returned to Vernon, Charlie helped his mother-in-law manage the Panhandle Hotel and later took a job at the

Vernon Post Office. But not until he became maintenance supervisor for the Vernon Cotton Oil Mills did he taste vocational contentment. Trouble-shooting among the thirteen cotton gins in the region helped gratify the love for mechanical engineering which, along with his family and music, formed the only real interests in Charlie Teagarden's life.

Ninety per cent of the Texas cotton crop was feeding overseas markets and fetching a high price. Vernon was already a major centre in the industry although the town owed its recent origin to cattle rather than cotton. Its early years were colourful and often violent. Their echoes had not quite faded when the Teagardens arrived.

The region still abounded in 'only yesterday' yarns of the Western Trail, the Chisholm and the Goodnight-Loving Trail. Just beyond the Red River, Comanche veterans, confined and subdued, recalled the battles of less than three decades ago. But just as the buffalo and the Indian retreated before the westward march of the ranchers and railroads so the mood and lore of the Plains foundered as State education and small-town culture joined honourable commerce to stamp each community with urban refinement.

The lives of the townsfolk were centred around church, school and the price of wheat, cattle and cotton. Music was their chief form of leisure. And in Vernon, Texas, in the infant years of the century, music meant Paul Goetze.

The Iowa Park music teacher moved to Vernon soon after the Geingars arrived there. In a short while Goetze was applying the benefits of classical training and discipline to those citizens with a natural bent for music. He was born near Leipzig in 1875 and had appeared before concert audiences at the age of five. Moreover, his talents extended to composition. Such was his impact upon Vernon that many of the parents who ushered their children into the Goetze study stayed for instruction themselves. Each music night Main and Wilbarger Streets, at whose intersection stood the Panhandle Hotel, rang with young voices as the Geingar quintet, Barbara, Goldie, Edna, Mary and Helen, emerged to attend their lessons. Later, Helen brought her husband along too. While the girls practised the piano, he struggled with a cornet.

If Charlie Teagarden lacked a keen ear for music and a sense of rhythm he possessed an unlimited stock of perseverance. Loving music, he was wholly aware of his shortcomings. Yet at no time did he yield to despair. When Vernon formed a town band under the leadership of Goetze, Charlie at first hesitated about joining it. But after some persuasion from Helen he bought a new Lyon and Healy cornet and went along to the courthouse.

For it was on the top floor of the Vernon Courthouse that the band rehearsed. Their uniforms were provided by the tycoon W. T. Waggoner and they gave summer evening concerts in the square pavilion. The organization included several respected citizens whose musical enthusiasms were not always matched by their skill. This produced a measure of relief to young Charlie and in a short while his playing improved noticeably.

On a burning August day in 1905, the Teagarden's first-born was christened. Aunt Barbara selected his name. She was an avid reader of popular novels and when her sister's child arrived she was under the spell of a particularly gallant hero named Weldon Leo.

'What shall we call him?' asked Helen.

Barbara was deep in her book. 'Weldon Leo,' she murmured without looking up. Her sister and Charlie exchanged nods of approval. The baby bellowed his protests but was overruled. Five years later he was still uneasy about it but more important matters were on his mind. He was playing scales on the tenor valve-horn and the piano. Neighbours were calling at the house asking to hear 'little Weldon' play sentimental waltzes for them. Soon, the Sunday afternoon music sessions at the Teagardens became a regular Mesquite Street function.

Weldon was not nearly so impressed by the arrival of a baby sister as he was by the gift of a trombone, although the occasion destroyed his dream of Santa Claus. He discarded the tenor horn, examined the trombone impassively for a while, then endeavoured to manipulate the slide. His arms were exasperatingly short. They remained short for several more years. As a result he achieved considerable skill in 'faking' notes beyond his reach. The habits imposed upon him by his limited armlength accompanied him into adulthood. They accounted for his economical employment of the slide, a departure from the excessive reaches which had become traditional to jazz trombone.

Like his father, Weldon displayed a strong instinct for machinery and Charlie took him on several short trips to the cotton gins. Weldon's interest, however, was more operational than passive and on one occasion, while his father's attention was elsewhere, he set the gin in motion. Charlie turned and proceeded to upbraid a quite innocent engineer standing near by. Calmly, Weldon studied the whirring gin with rapt attention.

His absorption in things mechanical was rewarded with gifts of a toy oil derrick, steam engine and erector set. These shared with the trombone his utter devotion. If he looked up at all from his possessions and wondered aloud what the neighbourhood kids were doing, his father silenced him immediately.

Charlie, in fact, seemed more alert to his duties as guardian rather than parent. He discouraged contact with other children, and forbade any when they failed to meet the social standards which he deemed proper. To enforce this policy he built a fence around the house. This increased the child's shyness, while reducing his capacity for outdoor games. On the other hand, it strengthened his concentration upon music and mechanics. Except during the unexpected visits of Uncle Will. Charlie Teagarden's fence couldn't keep out Uncle Will, though sometimes he wished it could. His hopes of protecting 'little Weldon' from undesirable influences vanished whenever Uncle Will rode in.

Will Geingar was Helen's only brother. Hard-working but unpredictable, he disappeared from home at the age of fifteen to return three months later draped in an Indian blanket and reciting lurid stories of the Comanches with whom he had been spending the time. Then off he went again, this time to drill oil for the Waggoners. He spent most of his adult years wild-catting through the south-west. Weldon may have been deprived of the fun of acting adventure stories with the neighbourhood kids. But he got them first hand from Uncle Will.

Charlie winced at Will's back-slapping manner, tipped-back hat and the frayed rope which served as a trouser belt. Weldon worshipped him. Once, over his father's objection, the boy was permitted to accompany Uncle Will on a trip to Colorado Springs. He took his trombone along and entertained the train passengers for nickels. Uncle Will added a couple of dollars and they bought a snare drum and a set of steel bells. As the Teagardens objected to any parlour demonstrations of Weldon's percussive ability, he hauled the equipment to school where he swapped clanging rhythms with the recess bell as the kids stomped in and out.

Charlie often expressed the fear that his son would grow up to be like Uncle Will. For the life of him Weldon was unable to regard the possibility as dreadful. But neither was he able to gauge the strength of his father's sense of neatness and propriety although he was reminded of it often enough.

In Charlie's view, the cause of every disaster that ever happened could be traced to somebody's oversight or slovenliness. He found enough evidence in the cotton gin shops to corroborate his view. Once, across the state line in Davison, Oklahoma, a gin blew up, killing the whole gang. Charlie was sent to investigate. One of the victims still clutched the steam throttle, his sightless eyes staring at a water gauge which showed the presence of water.

'But,' said Charlie later to his son, 'there was no water. The gauge was faulty, dirty. Someone had neglected to clean it.' In case Weldon was insufficiently impressed by this account, his father recruited bigger, weightier events to support his gospel of perfectionism. The spring of 1912 gave him the biggest of them all.

'You see,' he told his son that April night, 'it was all figured out not to sink. Perfect, or so they thought. But somebody, somewhere, slipped up. So the *Titanic* sank.'

Charlie's insistence upon perfection was directed not only at his son but within himself. Only when he placed the cornet to his lips was he reminded of the one chronic imperfection which he suffered. He never gave a sign of the frustration which welled in him at those times but Helen sensed it.

Meanwhile, Weldon rapidly mastered the essentials of the trombone. Of all musical instruments, it alone had remained basically unmodified since the Middle Ages. The fact gravely impressed him. The absence of valves or keys, the peculiar demands made upon the player's sense of pitch challenged him no less excitingly than the prospect of competitive sports confronting the boys from whom he was so effectively segregated by his father's fence. He would put the instrument down only to do household chores. Sometimes he had to watch his baby sister Norma, but even that task provided opportunity for practice.

Norma was exposed to the charms of the Teagarden trombone at a tender age. She showed a particular relish for *Goodbye, My Love, Goodbye* and would close her eyes peacefully during the second chorus. Thinking she was asleep, her brother would investigate other melodies. A squeal from the crib would hurry him back to *Goodbye, My Love, Goodbye*.

Paul Goetze was soon impressed by Weldon's musicianship. When Helen suggested that the boy take formal trombone tuition Goetze expressed frank doubts. 'He already knows,' said the German teacher, 'far more than he could be taught.'

Weldon's fame spread beyond Mesquite Street. He played solos with piano accompaniment in church and so charmed one member, who was also a merchant, that he equipped the boy with a linen suit (two pairs of trousers) and a cap. Someone else gave him a stool on which to rest his horn because he wasn't yet strong enough to hold it for long periods. His talents were also sought by the High School Girls' Band to which he, the only male member, contributed capably if woodenly.

He became the youngest member of the Paul Goetze Band when he was eleven; and although he had trouble keeping up with his colleagues' adult stride during Vernon street marches, his playing never lagged. Indeed, at weekly rehearsals, the occasional fumbling of less adroit members of the orchestra would shatter both his patience and shyness. Several times, in a bold piping voice which bore no trace of the later, familiar huskiness, he offered criticism. It was invariably met with annoyed reminders that small boys should be seen and not heard. (Except, of course, when they played trombone.) Anyway, the older musicians added, young Weldon wasn't exactly fault-less. Repeatedly, Paul Goetze had found it necessary to censure him for straying from the written music.

'The composer would prefer that you play the work as he wrote it,' Goetze would say softly. But to no avail. Trills, glides and what Goetze once described as 'other things not in the score' kept creeping into the boy's playing. The spirit of free improvisation was already stirring within him and neither Paul Goetze's gentle admonitions nor all the frowns of Vernon's most eminent citizens could daunt it.

Weldon walked home after rehearsal, trombone case firmly grasped, his rather plump face wearing a sober expression. Passers-by would look twice at a man carrying a horn case. For a boy they would practically get off the sidewalk and bow.

He was unsure how to react to his neighbours' admiration and usually sought brief escape from it over a soda in Pendle-ton's Drug Store. Sometimes he bought an extra one for Cathy Pierce, a member of the High School Band on whom he had a temporary crush. Cathy enjoyed a position of distinction among the town's younger set. Her father was the first Vernon citizen to own a car.

At school Weldon worked hard and did particularly well in arithmetic. He was later informed that he needn't have worried anyway. His popularity as a young musician would have carried him easily through all his grades. But at home he sensed a new perplexity, without fully comprehending it. His father still fought a frustrating battle with the cornet and to this dilemma was now added his son's precocity. Weldon was becoming in-creasingly sensitive to his father's musical imperfection and Charlie knew it.

Because of the long hours spent at the cotton gins Charlie

often practised before leaving the house at seven in the morning. His laboured efforts would awaken the boy who would writhe in his bed and shudder at each sour note. At times, he could not refrain from shouting a correction when his father faltered. Then Charlie was torn between gratitude and humiliation. Their relationship had never fully developed and now an element of strain entered it. The father was in his thirties, young enough to be a hopeful, albeit with a struggling hope. But the more evident his son's prowess became, the more dishearteningly clear were his own weaknesses.

Yet there was always room for paternal pride. When Weldon accomplished a faultless solo, though his own attempts miscarried, Charlie's pleasure was evident and unbounded. The pain of his failure was concealed. This was an inner, personal conflict and Charlie never allowed it to reach the dimension of a domestic crisis. On the contrary, a current of contentment ran through life on Mesquite Street.

It was true that the pages of the *Vernon Times* told of widespread unrest. References to Pershing and punitive expeditions and Pancho Villa were scattered through dispatches from an area of turbulence less than half a thousand miles to the southwest. From Europe came a never-ending flow of bloodstained bulletins. But these dark tidings seemed less real to the citizens of Vernon than the summer dust storms out of the Panhandle and the snowladen northers of deep winter; and when such winds swept through Mesquite Street, their fury only emphasized the security and contentment as the neighbours assembled indoors.

Helen sat at the piano, still young and pretty. At her side stood Weldon, black hair parted right down the middle, brown eyes serious above his trombone. Just behind her stood her husband, stocky, blond and anxious as he held the cornet to his lips.

Often Helen sang. The ballads were heavily sentimental and included one particularly fierce tear-jerker called *In the Baggage Coach Ahead*. This epic dealt with the sad railroad journey of a husband accompanying his late wife's coffin. Maudlin as it sounds today nobody then felt like laughing at it. Indeed, the family was sometimes moved to tears. Weldon would rescue them with a tune called *Laughing Sam* which may best be left to the imagination. Or Helen would switch to something like *Tickled to Death* or *Possum and Taters*, an ebullient pair of piano rags written by the long forgotten Charlie Hunter. *Maple Leaf Rag* was also highly popular in the area, due possibly to the composer Scott Joplin (himself a Texan) having taken his infectious rags all over the state. But pathos rather than frivolity ruled these family sing-songs and its traces, colouring voice and trombone, would linger far into Weldon's adult life; a reminder of what he would call, in retrospect, his moody childhood.

One morning he was told to go to the house of a neighbour instead of home after school. When he got there he was asked, 'Guess what you have in your house?'

Weldon's face puckered. Then, 'A dog?' he said hopefully. When they told him it was a baby brother he burst into a rare flood of tears.

The baby was christened Charles and Weldon got his dog. It was a hound of obscure pedigree and they named her Brownie. Brownie assumed a most protective role when the infant Charles developed a tendency to crawl out of the house and head for the railway track. Repeatedly, Brownie followed, nuzzling him off his course and thereby placing a million future jazz fans who consider Charles Teagarden a highly gifted trumpet player in her debt.

On rare occasions the family left Vernon for brief visits to the Reverend Renfrew's farm, just across the Red River in Oklahoma. Here, playing baseball with the Renfrew boys, Weldon realized just how hopeless at outdoor sports his enforced abstinence in Vernon had made him. The Renfrews soon vanished from Weldon's memory, with the exception of the eldest lad who bore the name Zenith and cheerfully embarrassed his reverend father by organizing Sunday sandlot games.

In the summer of 1918, despite a coolness with which certain citizens of Vernon appeared determined to regard him for the duration of the war, Paul Goetze held three students' recitals in the First Baptist Church. The third concert featured the orchestra which consisted of six violins, one flute, one clarinet, two cornets, a double bass, trap drums, two pianos, a pipe organ and a trombone.

The programme included *Homestead Melodies*, *Favourite French Songs*, *The Bohemian Girl* and excerpts from *Il Trovatore*. They could be guaranteed to defeat even young Teagarden's efforts to introduce 'other things not in the score'.

Far removed from Verdi and company, another kind of musical adventure was discovered by Weldon that summer. Since the Civil War and the rise of the cotton industry, Negroes had entered Texas in ever-increasing numbers. Their reception was not too friendly. The grim warning sign, 'Nigger, don't let the sun set on you,' was to be seen in many Texan towns. Large numbers of Negroes led a nomadic existence. Some followed lonely paths, like Blind Lemon Jefferson or the proud giant Leadbelly who rode the Texas railroads in 1918 singing his defiance of Jim Crow. Others were drawn together by the common impulse of religion to pitch their tents on the outskirts of town, rouse up the night with hymn shouts and handclaps, pray and weep and fold their tents and move on to the next town.

One such camp meeting lasted most of a week on a spare plot of ground near the railway track at the bottom of Mesquite Street. After sundown chanted spirituals soared to the evening sky and along Mesquite Street some listened half in wonderment; others closed their windows with emphasis. Each night Weldon crept out of the house to climb up on the fence and listen. A magic fell upon him and once he left his perch to venture within a few feet of the tent with its great shivering shadows cast by the lamps within. There he heard and felt the song and passion of a forlorn people.

His instinct for improvisation had already been stirred and was obeyed each time he pressed his lips to the trombone's mouthpiece. Now another vital, hitherto latent instinct was aroused—a feeling for the beat. There is a step in the evolution of every jazz musician when the spring is released, the indefinable response to *beat* awakened.

It came to young Teagarden in the rhythmic handclaps, the laments and hosannas of half a hundred Negro voices. It came from a tawdry tent, grey and shapeless under the Texas stars. Long after he had gone to bed its swinging pulse kept him throbbing all night while his mind built new and exciting melodic patterns.

In November 1918 during the week when Charlie Teagarden was to register for the draft, the 'flu epidemic struck him down. He was thirty-nine. He passed into a delirium. From his pale lips fell praise for his son's musical prowess. The words were broken but pride strengthened the voice which uttered them. It carried no hint of his own defeats. Near his bed rested the cornet he had never quite mastered. It was silent now and forever.

They came from miles around for the funeral. Some came in on the old Frisco railroad, a feeble track which crossed the Red River to end at Bugscuffle Station. The Red was in flood. Any moment, it was feared, the bridge might collapse. So the train halted and its passengers, dressed in black, alighted to cross the river carefully on foot. At Bugscuffle they were met by Cathy Pierce who drove them to Vernon in her father's car. She was propped by two pillows so she could reach the steering wheel.

So Mesquite Street mourned Charlie Teagarden while the world beyond rejoiced over the end of the First World War.

Helen was widowed at twenty-seven. She now had four children, a third boy, Clois, having arrived two years before her husband's death. The insurance money barely met funeral costs, and unpaid bills accumulated. Weldon assisted in their dissolution by servicing defunct gasoline pumps at Brad Hancock's garage and restoring them to their owners at a sizeable profit.

His father's passing removed most of the restrictions from him and he was aware of a new sense of freedom. It came too late to completely erase the diffidence which was by now part of his nature.

Tillie Geingar, meanwhile, was still active in the restaurant business and presently in California. But upon hearing of her son-in-law's death, she sold out, moved back to Vernon and helped Helen adjust herself to life without Charlie.

It was not long before Tillie found herself hankering after her chosen profession. Following a quick survey, she decided that catering prospects in Vernon were slender, moved the whole family to Oklahoma City and opened a restaurant. But although its sign bore the bold invitation '15 Cents Per Meal. All You Can Eat', the daily menu seldom offered more than bread, pies and cakes.

Unable to afford expensive equipment, Tillie and her daughter kneaded the dough by hand and baked it in a crude oven. Each morning, Norma and Charles were loaded with loaves and pastries and dispatched on a door-to-door sales mission. Weldon took a job in automobile service station where the boss strove to keep him out of the customers' sight. No driver, the boss felt, would risk handing over his precious Stutz to the care of a fourteen-year-old.

Despite the demands of the bakery, Helen successfully completed a music teachers' course; and when her brother-in-law wrote from his real estate office in Chappel, Nebraska, offering aid and the use of one of his houses, she gathered up her children and moved north. Her advertisement for pupils attracted about twenty children. Their progress was hampered by noisy interruptions from Norma and Clois. The two had reached the age of belligerency and were inclined to use their mother's music room as a battleground. Understandably, the pupils' attendance fell off.

It became necessary for Helen to seek extra income and she found it ($4 a night) in the rusty pit of Chappel's only cinema where she played the piano and was accompanied at week-ends by her son. For the Pearl White serials she banged out *The Ride of the Uhlans* while Weldon, at some loss how to match with a trombone the jerky flickering action on the screen, brayed loudly and pointlessly.

He was more at ease during the melodramatic sentimentalities of the sisters Gish or Talmadge. Then he would launch into several choruses of *Silver Threads* or *Oh, Dry Those Tears* which his mother would embroider with delicate piano chords. Sometimes he rested his horn, climbed into the projection booth at the rear of the cinema and operated the machine. He was particularly fascinated by the early master of screen derring-do, Eddie Polo, and became so engrossed in his exploits that he often forgot to change the reels.

The Teagarden family could afford little for protection against the freezing Nebraskan winter. On the coldest nights they all huddled together in the same bed with a pet collie dog serving as an extra blanket. Financial difficulties worsened and Helen's brother-in-law was unable to fulfil his promise of help. So once more she packed her small possessions and the family headed south to Oklahoma City.

Shortly after his return, Weldon fell in with the drummer of a military band composed chiefly of Ninetieth Division dough-boys stationed at Fort Sill. At the leader's invitation Weldon moved in with them. The soldiers were chafing for discharge. Their impatience was relieved in boisterous escapades of which Weldon was a frequent victim. On the parade ground, garbed in an ill-fitting uniform and surrounded by war-toughened veterans, he was a natural target for ribaldry. He slept through every reveille and sometimes awoke to find himself imprisoned by a mountain of boots, rifles, knapsacks and mess kits heaped on his bunk.

The Fort Sill sojourn broke down some of his shyness. But certain army crudities had entered his speech. About that time the brother of one of his new-found friends died of narcotic poisoning. These were, to Helen, danger signals. She decided the boy might be less exposed to harmful influences if he stayed for a while with her late husband's sister in California. For his part, Weldon was more attracted to Charlie's brother in San Angelo. And when Helen gave him money for his ticket to California he bought one for San Angelo instead.

Uncle Joe Teagarden was a blacksmith in the Oriente Rail-road Yards and spare-time fiddle player at local hillbilly functions. Like his late brother, Joe's talents were limited. But unlike Charlie, he was supremely unaware of his limitations. To Joe Teagarden a frankly off-key *Darling Nellie Gray* was utter bliss. And so easy to attain; all you had to do was lift bow and fiddle and scrape one across the other.

But there was always room for novel accompaniment, Joe felt, eyeing his nephew's trombone eagerly as he welcomed him. The very next night he fiddled frantically but proudly at a San Angelo corn ball with Weldon beside him alternately blowing and wincing.

The boy found a job as a projectionist in the Crystal Theatre. One evening, on his way home to Uncle Joe's, he met a pretty, quiet-mannered telephone operator whose hours of duty seemed to coincide with his; he saw her repeatedly and at last mustered the courage to buy her a soda at the drugstore. He had always been ill at ease with girls and was now relieved to meet one who was, if anything, shyer than himself. He celebrated his confidence by asking her name. It was Ora Binyon.

Back in Vernon, Helen became alarmed as weeks passed without a word from her son. Finally she sought the aid of the police. When they found him, Weldon was hauled before a judge and given a lengthy lecture on a son's duty to write home to his mother. That night Weldon wrote. His letter was composed in a mood of penitence to which Uncle Joe contributed a fiddled medley of sentimental ballads sharing the common theme of Mother. When Helen read the letter she was a little overwhelmed by the expressions of remorse and the fervent promises of more regular correspondence. Her son was never more effusive.

It was just as well, for it was months before she heard from him again. Now the envelope bore a San Antonio postmark. Weldon had accepted an invitation to join Cotton Bailey's Band. Bailey, a hunchback drummer, was passing through San Angelo when the sound of Weldon's trombone caught his attention. After a short negotiation, Weldon packed his horn, bade brief good-byes to Uncle Joe and Ora, and set off with Bailey for San Antonio.

On the way, it grew clear that either Bailey nursed a private grudge against the name 'Weldon' or he was incapable of remembering it. When addressing the boy he would hesitate, then blurt out 'Joe'.

Weldon protested. He had often wished that his parents had resisted Aunt Barbara's choice of a name. Bailey's 'Joe' held even less appeal. 'Look,' he said, 'if you can't manage the name Weldon, why not try "Jack"? The suggestion confused them both for some minutes. Then Bailey said 'Jack'. He repeated it as if taking a couple of practice shots.

He nodded. 'Jack. That's it.' He prodded the boy forcefully. 'What the hell is wrong with Jack?'

So somewhere along the road from San Angelo to San Antonio, 'Weldon' was discarded. It seemed to the young trombonist that with it went the last ties to home. Weldon was Mesquite Street and Vernon High and the cotton gins. Weldon was Paul Goetze and the Waggoner band and his father's laboured perfectionism. He was Weldon no more. When they reached San Antonio, Bailey rounded up his band and said, 'Meet Jack Teagarden.'

Chapter II

THE band was a four-man group playing nightly in the Horn Palace, a roadhouse six miles out on the old South Loop. It was an ornate barn where moneyed ranchers threw extravagant parties and less affluent soldiers from near-by Brooks and Kelly Fields squandered their pay cheques.

The Palace was owned by a burly six-and-a-half footer named Bill Keilmann who had it built to house his massive collection of animal horns. They sprouted from every wall, hundreds of them, straight, curved, twisted and several feet in length. Their value was rumoured at around $300,000. Keilmann was justifiably proud of his horns. Notwithstanding, the more daring customers risked his anger by using them as racks to support umbrellas, beer buckets and even friends overcome by the local tequila. Rarely did the excesses of the patrons go beyond this, however, due mainly to Keilmann's physique and his dexterity with a brace of pistols.

Cotton Bailey's drumming was of the dull plodding variety. But a newcomer named George Hill added a linear, more fluid quality with his clarinet. Hill moved in with Teagarden and a lasting friendship was formed. They were on the stand nightly until 4 a.m. when they adjourned to the Black Cat for strawberry shortcake and fish. They shared an adolescent eccentricity for eating dessert before the main dish.

They went to bed after dawn, lowered the shades to the rising

sun and slept. They awoke about six in the evening for a breakfast of apple-pie, trout and tartar sauce, then prepared for the
Horn Palace. Theirs was a novel schedule, denied to most boys
of sixteen.

Cotton Bailey left, taking not only his ponderous tempi but
the piano player as well. Bailey was replaced by Bill Hiburger,
a lad from Paris, Texas. An even younger boy applied for the
piano job. He was Terry Shand from Uvaldo. The band
listened to his playing with approval.

'How old are you?' said Keilmann.

'Fourteen.'

'Fair enough.' Keilmann nodded. 'Get out of those short
pants into long ones and you're hired.'

Shand, Hill and Teagarden formed a spirited trio. It was
augmented by the arrival of Porter Trest, a husky, bespectacled
young man with a skilful command of the c-melody saxophone.
The quartet made an unusual impact. Ranchers on the town
looked up from their call-girl companions. Drunks emerged
from their tequila jugs and blinked soberly. The dancers
shuffled around the floor with renewed zest. And some of the
bursts of counterpoint from the stand were wild enough to add
new curls to Keilmann's forest of trophies.

Jazz was pure adventure to the Horn Palace boys. None of
them had heard any of the jazz and ragtime records just
beginning to flow into the limited city markets. No publicized
trends or predecessors' talents influenced them. Their origins
were rural. They lacked sophistication and training. Thus their
improvisations were more truly spontaneous. Each popular
tune, no matter how weak or drab in its written form, presented
a challenge to Teagarden and his colleagues. They fell upon
such material with relish if not always with technique.

Although the Horn Palace regulars were sometimes uncertain of just what the boys on the stand were trying to do,
they recognized initiative when they heard it. What was more,
they rewarded it. When the musicians split the week's kitty they
often pocketed amounts of seventy or eighty dollars each.

A violent episode interrupted this idyllic life. One April

midnight a man called Yeager entered. He had been ejected from the Palace by Keilmann a month earlier. Now, obviously seeking vengeance, he was back. Moreover, he had brought along several relatives to help him find it.

The band played happily to a crowded dance floor. Jack was breaking in a new trombone, a handsome small-bore horn with a six-inch bell. As the dancers recognized Yeager a chill settled upon everybody except the musicians. They continued to play with gusto. The Yeager kin separated to take up strategic positions in each corner. The dance floor emptied rapidly. This was unfortunate for Keilmann who, striding across the floor, offered an expansive target. A volley of shots rang out. Caught in a terrible crossfire from ·45 and ·38 calibre pistols, Keilmann fell. Bullets continued to thud into his huge body until a series of clicks indicated empty chambers.

Uproar followed. Those who rushed to Keilmann's aid collided with others seeking escape. The band's performance ended with an abrupt medley of discords and crashes. Jack, who had never quite forgotten the exploits of his movie idol Eddie Polo, flung himself off the stand and ran to the fallen Palace owner. Terry Shand, never a Polo fan, vanished through a rear exit. Unfortunately the momentum of his departure carried him blindly to another exit where he ran headlong into an emerging Yeager.

The man poked Shand's stomach with his gun. 'Remember, kid,' he snapped. 'You didn't see a thing, did you?'

'Not a thing,' agreed the piano player readily. The gunman pulled the trigger anyway. Luckily the weapon was empty.

Inside the Palace a chorus of yells rose from behind the bass drum where George Hill discovered young Hiburger drenched with thick red stuff. It took Hill ten minutes to assure the boy that he was not bleeding to death, that the mess was simply the contents of two jars of jelly shattered from their shelf by the Yeager barrage.

Keilmann astonished everybody by refusing to die although doctors were plucking bullets from him months later. Jack and Shand were informed that their testimony would be required in court. Hiburger left urgently and the band was without a drummer.

Business fell off at the Horn Palace and the band's income fell with it. To increase their anxieties Jack and Terry were finding scrawled, unsigned notes in their mailboxes. The gist was that it would be to everybody's benefit, including theirs, if they got out of town before the trial date. Jack's immediate reaction was to buy a Model-T Ford. He drove Shand out of San Antonio as far as Kelly Field where they were smitten by a sudden mood of bravado. Notes? Since when were they scared of threat notes? And how did they know the writer was not some harmless crank? These and similar comforting questions were raised and left unanswered on the dusty Laredo Highway as Jack steered the Model T into Kelly Field.

Shand's mother supervised a canteen on the Field. And here the boys sat, munching Mrs. Shand's pies and marvelling at the Orenco pursuit ships and Sopwith trainers winging overhead at speeds of 150 m.p.h. Then they drove back to town, saw Fatty Arbuckle in *The Dollar a Year Man* at the Royal and got to the Horn Palace late for work but carefree.

Next morning the notes appeared again. Their mood was uglier.

The boys were weighing them doubtfully when a phenomenal rainfall descended upon the area. Several creeks burst their banks. Jack was driving home from the Palace when the flood struck. He turned into Dallas Street as a torrent of water swept towards him bearing on its crest a confused looking sea lion. The flood had already hit downtown Antonio and invaded Breckenridge Park Zoo, liberating an assortment of animals.

The big flood took a heavy toll of life and paralysed San Antonio for weeks. Many buildings were wrecked. Among the casualties was the city courthouse. When word spread that the records of current or pending actions were destroyed, Teagarden and Shand heard the news with some relief. They marked the event by drinking tequila for the first time in their lives and spent much of the following day being dreadfully sick.

They had barely recovered when a letter arrived from George

Hill. He had left the Horn Palace band shortly after the Keilmann shooting, joined an unstable orchestra from West Texas
and was left broke and stranded in Galveston when the leader
disappeared with the musicians' wages. After living on beans
and coconut pie for over a week Hill found himself listening
one night to a dreary little ensemble which only came to life
when its xylophonist took solos.

Hill learned that the xylophonist was Peck Kelley and the
two met. At once Kelley bought Hill a huge dinner. He continued to feed him for the rest of the season. Then they went
to Houston and joined an orchestra led by Peck's uncle. Peck
was featured on the drums as well as the xylophone. Sometimes
he played the pipe organ at the Majestic Theatre. And now he
was forming his own band.

The letter from Hill was followed by a wire from Peck himself. His new band would bear the title Peck's Bad Boys and he
wanted Teagarden in it. Invitations were also extended to
Porter Trest and Shand. As Kelley had now decided to concen-
trate upon the piano it was agreed that Shand would take the
drummer's chair.

Teagarden and his friends were excited, for reports of Peck's
piano virtuosity had already reached them, but as their train
pulled out of San Antonio that afternoon in late 1921 they could
have had no awareness of the legend which the next two
decades were to weave around Peck Kelley of Houston.

Chapter III

By the middle of the twentieth century jazz had become a respectable subject. Magazines which regarded it earlier as a dirty word, now carried forums debating progressive trends and past influences in the music. Several popular magazines explained hot jazz and in 1955 *Good Housekeeping* described (not without a struggle) cool jazz. The faces of jazz musicians appeared on the covers of national periodicals. Jazz, it was said repeatedly, had arrived.

Its journey had been highlighted by several colourful legends told so often that the colour was beginning to tarnish. The mid-century public which approached jazz with intellectual curiosity seemed unimpressed by the oft-told tales of Bix's habits, Buddy Bolden's roaring madness and the whorehouses of Storeyville.

One legend persisted. It is unique in jazz because of its quietness, its very absence of lurid eccentricity. But upon every cursory examination it ceases to be legend. The dictionary defines 'legend' as an unauthenticated story handed down by tradition and popularly regarded as historical. Peck Kelley's story is contemporaneous and easily authenticated—although he never cut a commercial record in his life and rarely leaves his native Houston. Many outstanding musicians have heard him play. Some describe his performance with superlatives. From expert opinions it is safe to assume that Kelley is, or was at one time, a fine, even a great, pianist. The puzzle of Peck

Kelley rests solely on his lifelong abhorrence of fame and fortune.

It was Teagarden who first brought word of Peck Kelley north, east and west. He never spoke of him without a certain reverence and affection. For Teagarden there is no Peck 'legend'. Peck is an honest man, a brilliant pianist and a great friend. His only hatred is for sham and exploitation. To the trombonist, it is all as simple as that.

Of course, it isn't enough. There was more than a hint of hero worship in Jack's early relationship with Kelley. Not only was he the polished band leader. To his Bad Boys and through Jack's eyes particularly, he often effected a paternal role. For example, whenever they were in danger of being fleeced by dice racketeers on the Houston-Galveston circuit, Kelley would enter the game, restore the boys' losses with several brisk flourishes of the dice and dismiss them with stern warnings against the follies of gambling.

Thereafter, Jack nourished a devotion to Peck which strains the credibility of his appraisal. Moreover, Jack has always suffered from an inability to discuss other people's faults. Indeed, he will conceal his awareness of them and tend to overpraise virtues. This trait is frequently exasperating and not always fair to those in question.

So the Teagarden verdict on Peck is unsatisfactory, taken alone. But there is no lack of unprejudiced comment. Big band leaders, past and present, have sought after Peck. Ben Bernie and Jimmy Dorsey. Rudy Vallee and Tommy Dorsey. Paul Whiteman and Bob Crosby. Offers have been generous, though no more remarkable than $1,500 per week and a white grand piano in Chicago's Sherman Hotel.

Peck refused them all. The manner of his refusal varied only slightly. 'Hots, I'm not ready yet....' Or, 'I'm not good enough.' Or, 'I've got two good cigars a day, three meals and a piano. I'm content.' When Teagarden aroused Bing Crosby's interest in the pianist, the singer agreed to hear him. Peck was sent for. 'Sorry,' said Peck. 'I've got nothing to play for Bing.'

Alec Templeton called the man who had nothing to play for Bing, a 'unique figure'. Rhodes Cook, a Texas music teacher and author, says flatly, 'I don't believe a more consummate artist ever lived.'

When Ben Pollack, the veteran bandleader and tough businessman, went down to Houston convinced that Kelley was an overrated screwball, he returned with this opinion. 'It doesn't seem possible that a man can live and play as much piano as he played that morning—a man would have to practice thirty-six hours a day. I finally heard someone play piano as I thought it should be played. But,' Pollack added, 'I never dreamed anyone could play ten times that much.'

John Dickson Kelley was born in 1898 and though no introspective problem child he lacked the wildness of his five brothers. Two of them drowned in Buffalo Bayou, at the back of their Houston home. How Peck got his nickname is a mystery but an unimportant one. The kids he grew up with bore even odder titles like Cabbage Barnett and Red Dog Johnson. When Peck was five the family moved to the house on State Street which was to be Peck's home for the rest of his life.

His parents had an upright piano in the house but were not very musical. Peck himself was unimpressed by formal instruction and sought greater stimulation listening to Negro pianists in the gin dives. At eighteen he enjoyed a local reputation as party piano player and sometimes as a singer in street-corner quartets. For a while he cleaned floors at Big Ed Payne's Southern Dinner Club, was less preoccupied with mop and pail than with the piano, and drew frequent tongue-lashings from the boss. Years later Big Ed hired Peck as his top attraction.

Following a brief interlude in the West Texas oilfields, Peck Kelley returned to music. The idea of forming his own band had already occurred to him when he met George Hill. He was soon impressed by Hill's account of the Horn Palace boys, particularly his praise of the trombonist, and decided they should form the core of his first band.

When Teagarden and Shand arrived in Houston they made straight for Joe Ludwig's house as instructed by Peck's wire. Kelley was engaged to Joe's daughter Dooley, and arrangements had been made for the newcomers to stay at her home. There

Teagarden met Peck for the first time. The pianist was seven years Jack's senior, rather short, slim and dark. His voice and manner, like his clothes, were smooth and precise. He smiled often, but there was an air of understatement about him even then.

It persisted at the piano although eloquence flowed from the keys he touched. Only occasionally did he appear moved by his own playing. His inner feelings were well masked. The first time he played for Teagarden he stole a couple of glances at the awed youth, let one thick eyebrow lift a little and smiled. Teagarden shook his head in disbelief. The flashing changes of mood, the unpredictable paths of improvisation, the rolling intensities of jazz and the not incongruous quotations from classics the boy had never heard of—*this* was strange and exciting piano playing. There were blues qualities, too, no doubt acquired by Peck from his early contact with Texas Negroes. These had a profound effect upon the young trombonist from Vernon.

Rehearsals had not been a regular feature of the Horn Palace days and when Peck called for a morning workout in the local Elk's Hall, Shand and Teagarden protested. But Peck proved a speedy inspiration and the gathering was a happy one. Indeed a rapport was formed among Peck's Bad Boys which later personnel modifications failed to destroy. Jack and Kelley would indulge in some hair-raising trombone-piano duets in the course of which Teagarden might suddenly pause, shout his admiration for Peck, then continue blowing. Half-way through the next chorus Peck would reciprocate in like manner. This practice both amused and exasperated the rest of the group and was referred to generally as 'cutting a frog'.

The following summer, when the band worked at the Tokyo Gardens Pavilion in Galveston, Peck quietly announced the date of his and Dooley's wedding. The Bad Boys were instantly loud with congratulations. Jack's were edged with a slight doubt. During their stay with the Ludwigs, both he and Shand had grown apprehensive of Dooley's loyalty to their beloved boss. They hadn't voiced their fears. Peck was plainly in love.

Furthermore, they were mere kids whose conclusions on adult relationships might not have been seriously heeded. But a few nights after the marriage Jack was strolling along the moonlit beach when he came across Peck sitting forlornly on the sea wall. Jack joined him. They sat in silence for several minutes, looking out over the Gulf. Suddenly Peck made a short remark concerning Dooley which underlined Jack's earlier doubts. The pianist spoke quietly, firmly and with finality.

Shand left Peck's Bad Boys and was replaced by Reginald Gullick. The band also included Gilbert O'Shaughnessy on the clarinet, and occasionally an ex-sailor named Walt Holtzhaus. Holtzhaus was a skilful trumpet player who paired with Jack in many experimental duets. Encouraged by Peck, they achieved some startling effects using quart beer-cans as mutes or 'growlers'. Unfortunately these pioneer endeavours went unrecorded. However, it was at this time that Jack evolved an unusually haunting 'jug' tone by substituting an ordinary water glass for the bell of his trombone. The moody sound, so expressive of the blues, later developed into an important Teagarden trademark.

George Hill's mother arrived in Galveston that summer and decided that her son and his companions could use a little parental control, not to mention home cooking. So she rented a furnished cottage and Hill and Jack moved in. Holtzhaus followed. At his heels came Porter Trest. The tenants of Hill Cottage were about to close the door when Gullick showed up carrying his bass drum. Gullick had also acquired a wife. It was pointed out to him that the already crowded cottage could not possibly take both drums and wife. After a whispered debate with Mrs. Gullick the drummer shrugged ruefully, left his trappings outside and ushered his bride within.

It was a happy summer. Post-war boom money flowed lavishly. The Tokyo Gardens Pavilion was elegantly set within a pleasure park called Joyland. It was packed nightly. Gentle breezes floated in off the warm Gulf. Giant crystal balls hung from the ceiling, revolved and flashed a myriad colours. Prohibition was barely three years old and bootleg liquor not yet generally available. Any sparkle on the faces of the youths foxtrotting with their ladies sprang from 1922's prosperity or over-consumption of ginger beer.

The band played *Ain't We Got Fun, Aggravatin' Papa, The Sheik, Dancing Fool, My Buddy* and *Toot, Toot, Tootsie*. The dancers jigged cheerfully around the floor and were only momentarily upset by the fitful symptoms of agitation from the bandstand. Jack then would compose them with an instrumental solo, *Love Brings a Little Gift of Roses*.

When their escorts weren't looking some of the girls gazed a little dreamily at the trombonist. They forgave his tendency to desert the melody and paid more heed to his pleasing smile, dark eyes, and glossy black hair parted just off-centre. But while he was not ignorant of this attention it failed to rival his continued interest in more mechanical attractions. He didn't enthuse much over electricity—working parts intrigued him more than invisible forces. But the advent of radio encouraged him to build crystal sets for Mrs. Hill and her charges. It also provided a reasonable excuse for clambering over the roof tiles to erect an aerial. His housetop activities produced several small leaks which Mrs. Hill overlooked, reflecting no doubt that not every house in the neighbourhood had a trombone playing boarder. Nor, indeed, a crystal set.

Jack was by now becoming aware of the directions other jazz musicians were taking. He briefly encountered such Texas strolling groups as the Powder River Boys, Jimmy Joy and his Sole Killers, Buddy's Blue Melody Band and the Texas Jazzers of Austin. But of developments beyond the state he was utterly oblivious until records of Phil Napoleon's Memphis Five and the New Orleans Rhythm Kings came his way. His feeling for the blues, unique among white musicians, was already stirring. It awakened fully one night in a shabby theatre on the north side of the town when, tears blurring his eyes, he heard Bessie Smith sing *Cold in Hand* and a number of other blues. Then, his mind phrased the responses his trombone would convey behind Bessie in a recording studio, ten years later.

During a season at the Sylvan Beach Park on Galveston Bay,

the band suffered a minor crisis involving Porter Trest. The
c-melody man's limited vision tempted the more sportive of
the Bad Boys to such pranks as assuring him falsely of the
absence of a curb and watching him trip on his face. Trest
finally lost patience and after listening to some of Holtzhaus's
tales of the sea he quit the band and got himself hired on a
local ferry boat.

Remorse clouded the musicians' lives until Trest sheepishly
and unexpectedly returned. His job, he explained, had been to
straighten the anchor chain when the vessel hauled anchor. As
this operation took place in the near darkness of the vessel's
hold, Trest became quite lost. He managed to twist the chain
into a series of kinks and was slowly strangling himself with it
when two crew members arrived to extricate him. By then they
had reached dry land where Trest promptly and gratefully
accepted the captain's invitation to leave the boat.

The composition of Peck's Bad Boys was never stable beyond
a few months. Departures and arrivals continued to mark the
organization's progress. That the musical output remained high
in quality was due chiefly to Kelley's shrewdness in selecting
replacements. Not only did he bar mediocrity, he sought
originality and was able to distinguish it from mere novelty.

One of the most original artists ever to perform under the
supervision of Kelley or anyone else stepped off the train in
Houston station and glanced nervously around. He wasn't all
that far from his home town of St. Louis, but sixteen-year-old
Charles 'Pee Wee' Russell was already homesick. For comfort
he reached into the pocket of his brand new suit and fingered
the telegram which had enticed him from his chair in Herbert
Berger's Cordova Hotel Orchestra.

He straightened his derby and gazed anxiously at his new
spats. Then he felt someone else staring at them. He looked up.
Peck Kelley was studying him with disbelief. After terse introductions they got in a car and drove off. For some minutes the
journey was painful. Peck's lips didn't move but his eyes were
asking, *What the hell is this?*

The purpose of Pee Wee's freshly-bought finery had been to

impress, certainly. But the reaction of his new boss was not the one he had expected. Peck clearly needed swift reassurance. Pee Wee gave it. He took off his derby and without a word flung it through the window. Then he looked at Peck—and relaxed. Peck was grinning.

But Pee Wee's misery returned when they reached Goggin's Music Store. Peck made straight for the piano and began to play the blues. The blues was Pee Wee's music too and he felt an instant kinship. He was also convinced he could never meet Peck's stern requirements. And not only was he just not good enough but he didn't have the train fare back to St. Louis. Peck kept building chorus on chorus while Pee Wee's lean body slumped.

Jack Teagarden came in, took up his horn and joined Peck. Pee Wee muttered 'Oh, Jesus', and wondered what the hitch-hiking chances were along the Texas-Missouri highways. When Teagarden hit his second chorus Pee Wee edged towards the door. Jack signalled him to play. Slowly Pee Wee's confidence struggled back; his apprehension escaped through his clarinet.

Thus Teagarden first heard the style now familiar to a generation of jazz lovers. Thin, reedy, agitated, so much like the man himself as to present a rare example of the oneness of music and personality. In the shadowy backroom of Goggin's Music Store, Peck and Teagarden listened and they knew it was good.

Peck's group was further enhanced by two New Orleans men of Italian extraction. One was the trumpeter Leon Prima. His companion was a slim pale master of a delicate clarinet style as disconcerting as the far-off light which sometimes glazed his eyes. His name was Leon Rapollo. With his wife and son he moved into a near-by beach cottage from which there soon arose the mingled aroma of garlic and marijuana. But sickness had not yet begun to twist the magic of Rapollo's clarinet. The shadow of the asylum was three years away.

Sometimes in the deepest hours of the night Rap put aside the clarinet in favour of the guitar. Out on the beach when the world had gone to sleep he would play a few chords to refresh his friends. Pee Wee would lift his clarinet and breathe the breath of jazz through it. Broken phrases emerged, soulful plaints alternating with wry proposals grittily voiced as if he hadn't shaken all the sand out. Prima caught the mood and blew his protests into the warm night. Then Teagarden emphasized their statements with powerful trombone passages, achieving a brazen shouting intensity which surprised even himself.

Thus they played till dawn. High over Galveston Bay, only the moon listened.

In late 1923 Jack accepted an offer to join the Doc Ross Jazz Bandits, a popular organization operating out of Wichita Falls. The chance of increased recognition, the certainty of improved salary, were factors weighing his decision. Against them was set the deep and happy comradeship he enjoyed with Peck Kelley.

Peck's spoken good-byes were brief and unsentimental. He said much more through his music. When Teagarden left the Bad Boys, uppermost in his mind were the sight and sound of Peck Kelley at the piano. In the turbulent years which lay ahead of the boy from Vernon the vision remained. Not always in the foreground but somewhere at the back of his thoughts, a faithful vision, the memory of long-forgotten joys. It served as a source of comfort during the time of the blues.

Throughout those years, what of Peck himself?

His non-working hours were spent more and more in the company of books and his parents. He read the Bible often and ventured into philosophy. Cars, radios, the trappings of the twentieth century made small impression on him. The only car he ever owned was stolen in 1927; and his report of the theft to the police was barely acknowledged. After some weeks Peck found the car—parked in front of the police station. Without a word he climbed in and drove off. Later the car vanished again. This time for good.

Kelley's response to the classical composers was genuine and immediate, but his knowledge was fragmentary. So he plunged into a lengthy study of Bach, Chopin and fundamental piano theory.

He emerged with a deeper humility and more flexible improvisory technique. But he continued to work in such places as the Tremont Café and the Rice Hotel, Houston.

And now the spotlight began to descend upon him. Ironically it coincided with a darkening of his vision due to glaucoma. His skill at the piano, however, remained unaffected. Someone up in New York wrote a song about him called *Beat Me Daddy, Eight to the Bar*. *Collier's Magazine* ran an article portraying him as an ungrammatical eccentric, a 'sad-eyed, soft-spoken master whom God jocularly fingered for genius'.

Purple prose, perhaps, but it *was* publicity; and the subsequent offers were tempting. Yet Peck considered them a nuisance, had his phone disconnected, and ignored all letters. Apart from his piano, his chief delights were playing tennis or chess—at which he excelled—and sitting for hours with ailing neighbours.

His struggle with glaucoma continued. Sometimes his doctors were optimistic, sometimes they forecast blindness. Their uncertainty, and that of all the world, seemed to leave him unmoved. But he yielded to occasional bursts of anger at what he considered the follies and falsities of the masses. As a close friend put it, 'For crowds Peck has only contempt. For individuals, warmth and humour. He loathes the public and loves people.'

When the public reached out for him in the early nineteen-forties he shrank angrily from it. To his relief, it ran true to form and ignored him when he resisted its blandishments. He last played for an audience in 1949 at the Dixie Bar, owned by the same Big Ed Payne who had employed him as a floor sweeper thirty years earlier.

When his parents died Peck was left alone. He had neither loved nor married since that far-off fiasco with Dooley Ludwig. Alone, he wasn't lonely. The touch of sadness to his smile might only be due to the passing of old familiar faces. For Peck now the precious things in life were the simple ones. The friendly gossip of neighbours. Solitary walks down to Lower Main. Sunlight on the porch of the house on State Street. And always, among the lengthening shadows, the piano and the memories.

Chapter IV

WHILE young Jack Teagarden approached a jazzman's maturity in Houston as one of Peck's Bad Boys, the opening shots in a militant anti-jazz campaign were being fired along scattered fronts up north. Few of the founding fathers of jazz alive today have much idea of the ferocity with which the 1922 attack upon their music was launched. Certainly they had no inkling at the time. Teagarden was ripping out his first blues phrases over Peck's rolling bass. Louis Armstrong had said farewell to New Orleans and was travelling 'up the country' to Chicago and King Oliver. Benny Goodman, at thirteen, was taking lessons in a Chicago slum from a German teacher of the clarinet.

Furthermore, the battle communiqués were issued by the attacking forces and appeared in periodicals which few young jazz musicians of the early 'twenties were likely to read intently —if at all. Had they done so they would have encountered such headlines as 'Unspeakable Jazz Must Go' and 'Does Jazz Put the Sin in Syncopation?' This might not have persuaded them to hurl their instruments away in despair. But lacking an articulate spokesman, they could not have mustered any kind of a passable defence. Twenty-five years hence, a self-appointed public relations man was to state the case for jazz musicians with heat if not always with eloquence. But Eddie Condon was a brash kid hanging around Friar's Inn to hear the New

Orleans Rhythm Kings when, in the same city, J. Louis Guyon
advocated the abolition of jazz.

This call came from an unexpected quarter. For Guyon was
Chicago's biggest dance-hall operator. Nevertheless, he pro-
claimed that anyone who said that the youth of both sexes can
mingle in close embrace without suffering harm, was a liar.
Parenthetically, he defined close embrace as 'limbs intertwined
and torsos in contact'.

'Add to this position,' he went on, 'the wriggling movements and the sensual stimulation of the abominable jazz
orchestra with its voodoo-born minors and its direct appeal
to the sensory centres, and if you can believe that youth is
the same after the experience as before, then God help your
child.'

As with dance-hall operators, so with dance teachers. 'These
moaning saxophones call out the low and rowdy instinct,' said
Fenton T. Bott, director of dance reform in the National
Association of Dancing Masters. 'The jazz is too often followed
by the joy ride. The lower nature is stirred up as a prelude to
unchaperoned adventure.'

Then Mr. Bott put in an advertising plug for a booklet (with
chart) which he had just issued showing the correct positions
for approved dances. Recommended by the United States
Public Health Service, the booklet warned against 'vulgar jazz
music' and urged dance teachers to forbid the touching of
cheeks, neckholds, shimmy and toddle.

Some cities employed policewomen to supervise public
dancing. Philadelphia appointed a lady to instruct seventy-five
policemen detailed for the enforcement of dancing regulations.
By the happiest of coincidences her name was Margurite Walz.
She advised Philadelphia's finest not to permit 'abdominal
contact or the Washington Johnny, in which the legs are
spread apart'.

The General Federation of Women's Clubs expressed horror
at the introduction of corset check rooms in many dance halls.
Thundered the Federation, 'Those under the demoralizing
influence of the persistent use of syncopation are actually

Vernon High School Band, 1917. Weldon (later Jack) Teagarden
is on the extreme left

Three of Peck Kelly's original Bad Boys on the beach at Galveston,
Gulf of Mexico in 1922

A rare photograph of Terry Shad, Jack Teagarden and (behind)
Pee Wee Russell, taken in 1923

incapable of distinguishing between good and evil, between right and wrong.'

The anti-jazz forces were not exclusively cranks. They included respected church and patriotic bodies. Their attack was wild and sweeping. All forms of dancing and dance music from the bunny hug to the waltz were 'jazz' and therefore immoral. The bored banjo player plunking nightly behind a violin whining *Margie* and the self-styled ragtime artists tinkling *Nola* were bracketed with the genuine creative musicians whose talents, buried in a thousand rackety dance-hall bands across the country, sometimes, somehow, burst forth with rare brilliance.

But all was jazz and therefore condemned. Being condemned it had to die. So Clive Bell, in the *New Republic*, announced, 'Jazz is dead, or dying at any rate, and the moment has come for someone who likes to fancy himself wider awake than his fellows to write its obituary notice. . . .'

If New Orleans was the cradle of jazz, it was already denying any claim to the title. The city's most powerful newspaper defined the music as, 'The indecent story, syncopated and counterpointed. . . .' Had dance music generally not been associated with, and even held responsible for, whatever loosening of moral restraints followed World War I, it is probable that its development would have been speeded and dignified. That it developed at all was due chiefly to the concomitant growth of the phonograph industry. Far removed from the sources of jazz, youngsters with latent gifts were influenced and encouraged by those musicians lucky enough to have access to recording studios.

In 1924 American homes had eight million phonographs. Three years later the innovation of electrical recording gave that figure a boost which was, however, shortlived. Depression and the spread of radio brought a slump to the industry in the early 'thirties. But during the hey-day of the phonograph, the gospel of American jazz was preached from the living-room victrola. In Texas, Jack Teagarden and Peck's other Bad Boys listened enthusiastically to Phil Napoleon's Memphis Five, the New

Orleans Rhythm Kings or early Louis Armstrong accompaniments to blues singers of the coloured vaudeville circuit. Up in Chicago, Benny Goodman and the talented scholars of Austin High received more personal inspiration from Bix Biederbecke and the Wolverines, Johnny Dodds and Armstrong.

Dance musicians of the early 'twenties were confronted with such popular songs as *When My Baby Smiles at Me*, *Swanee*, *Whispering*, *Avalon*, *Japanese Sandman*, *I Never Knew*, *When Buddha Smiles*, *Sheik of Araby*, etc. Although it was the fashion of the day to treat these with plenty of thumping 'razz-ma-tazz' or sensuous violins, as the mood dictated, the melody was more or less faithfully adhered to.

To Teagarden and his noncomformist contemporaries, this was of course unsatisfying. The indefinable impulses which set them apart from the run-of-the-dance-hall players resulted in some spectacular improvisations upon many trite tunes. These creative jazz musicians were too scattered to be described as a school. But their endeavours formed the mainstream of authentic jazz. And when the public, wearied by the rackety, acrobatic, comic-hatted 'jazz' or outraged by 'what it is doing to our children', eagerly accepted the slick refinements of the Paul Whiteman phase, that vital mainstream went underground but continued to flow.

Chapter V

EDWARD 'DOC' ROSS, an affable ex-farmer with a good head for business and a fondness for jazz drumming, placed no restraints upon his men. They inspired each other and imitated no one. The only music they read was written on a lead sheet which they studied, memorized, then threw away. The result was a lusty, free-wheeling music which made the Doc Ross Jazz Bandits one of the most sought-after bands in the south-west. Some of its members, like Bob McCracken (clarinet), Wilbur Stump (piano) and Cliff Ramey (trumpet) graduated into capable musicians who served in some of the best bands of the swing era.

The Jazz Bandits pursued an itinerary which would have baffled Rand-McNally. They played at theatres, dance halls, open-air shows, tank towns and saloons. They barnstormed every hamlet in Texas with a population over five hundred. Sometimes the number of bandsmen exceeded the number of people who showed up to dance.

Shortly after he joined the band, Teagarden got a call from San Angelo. It was Ora Binyon. Exchanges of affection were reaffirmed, this time with the boldness that only a long-distance telephone wire can prompt. Their conversation was overheard by an inquisitive but romantically inclined telephone operator who immediately spread the report that a wedding was imminent.

The young musician was known all over Texas. The shyly pretty Ora, though less widely famed, was well thought of in San Angelo. It was, everyone agreed before Jack had even proposed, a charming match. He journeyed to San Angelo and arrived at Ora's home as the presents were being delivered. Congratulations and gifts kept up their pressure until, slowly untying the ribbon from one of the wedding gifts, Jack Teagarden proposed.

They were married at the Binyon home early in 1923 and shortly afterwards Ora was introduced to the vicissitudes of life with a travelling musician. Brief but painful spells of loneliness alternated with hasty reunions in shabby hotel rooms and the vexations of living from a suitcase.

There were also the uncertainties of season lay-offs. During one, Jack received an offer to join Herbert Berger's band in St. Louis. There was a spot for piano, too, so he hunted up Terry Shand. Ora, who was seven months pregnant at the time, went along with them. Upon arriving they were told a local union rule barred them from playing. The news was disastrous. They had been relying upon a salary advance. Broke, without even funds to buy petrol for the drive back, they wandered over to the Union Hall where Shand hit upon an idea. Two hours later Jack was racking up balls on the pool table for him while Shand took on all comers at ten cents a shot. Ora waited quietly in the lobby of a drab hotel around the corner. She didn't have to wait very long. Shand and her husband drove up. 'All aboard,' drawled Jack. 'We're gassed up.' Their short-lived pool table partnership had paid off.

During another lay-off Teagarden journeyed to Wichita Falls and sat in with a small unit featuring Snaps Elliott (piano) and one Ross Majestic on the trumpet. After listening to him play they not only urged him to remain but offered to let him direct. He accepted, the personnel was increased to seven and, managed by a local backer named R. J. Marin, the Original Southern Trumpeters were formed. Their single outstanding triumph was the promotion of American jazz in Mexico.

The music had already crossed the border on radio waves

from the Dallas News Station. Hearing the Southern Trumpeters broadcast one night the American Consul-General in Mexico City was moved to express his delight. 'The gentlemen broadcasting,' he wrote, 'couldn't have been heard more distinctly had they been standing in our hall. . . .' As was the popular custom, telegrams containing requests were read over the air and the numbers obediently played. This further charmed the Consul-General who concluded with a tribute, in which his wife shared, to the band's rendition of *Angry* and *I've Got a Cross-Eyed Papa but he Sure Looks Straight to Me.*

So although radio sets in Mexico were few and far between, the country had to some degree at least been exposed to Yanqui jazz without noticeable effect upon U.S.-Mexican relations. In June 1924 the *Mexican-American* announced the 'invasion' of Mexico by the Southern Trumpeters. They could be seen at Abel's Restaurant on Avenida Juarez. 'Something new,' said the journal, 'is promised to frequenters of the restaurant. A feature of the orchestra is Mr. Jack Teagarden, claimed to be the South's Greatest Trombone Wonder.'

If this wasn't sufficient to lure hordes of Mexicans to the Avenida Juarez an extra bait was prepared by R. J. Marin. He claimed the distinction of receiving more letters and telegrams in answer to one night's broadcasting than had any orchestra in the entire U.S.A. since radio started. He cited a figure of six hundred and forty-two.

The Original Southern Trumpeters, who were also advertised as the South's Greatest Pep Artists, performed nightly. Abel's customers, described as the Smartest Crowd in Mexico, were charged two pesos each for tea dances and four pesos for dinner. On the stand the Trumpeters were elegant in tuxedos and black ties, their hair slicked back in the Valentino fashion of the day. Off duty they leaned more towards sweaters and sports attire. Jack particularly favoured a cap. If the peak were dented and the crown stained so much the better. Ora's efforts to cure him of his addiction to battered caps were feeble compared to those of later wives and acquaintances. None fully succeeded.

Snaps Elliott left the band and Terry Shand came south to occupy the piano chair. He brought his new bride Evelyn with him. As their marriage was only a few weeks old its novelty still stimulated them into all forms of horseplay. One afternoon while crossing the park they came to a puddle. Terry swept his wife into his arms and proceeded to carry her across. She struggled playfully but with force. Immediately a detachment of Mexican police bore down on them. Shand's Mexican was limited. The policemen knew no English. The piano player was marched off to jail where he remained until intervention from no less a source than the Mexican presidency (invoked by R. J. Marin) brought about his release.

Marin, though short and afflicted with an occasional stammer, was a vain man. He constantly used perfume and wore a toupee which never quite succeeded in its purpose of deception. One night, Jack and Shand, still celebrating the latter's release from jail, stole into Marin's bedroom—while he was asleep. Jack opened the window, leaned out and fired a gold-plated pistol which he had bought that afternoon as a souvenir. The noise attracted the ever-vigilant police who burst into Marin's room, switched on the light and stared at the gun which Jack had thoughtfully tossed on Marin's bed before leaving. Marin, aghast at being surprised without his toupee, jumped out of bed and was immediately seized. Struggling with his stammer, his meagre Mexican and his toupee, Marin provided several moments' entertainment for the guffawing Southern Trumpeters who by now were crowding his doorway.

But the Trumpeters' popularity tumbled sharply the night Dee Orr's brother showed up. Dee Orr was their drummer. His brother Frank, who was something of an impulsive vagrant, greeted the whole band warmly, and since it was July 4th insisted it play the *Star Spangled Banner*. Moreover, he demanded that everyone present stand at attention. Everyone did so following which the Mexicans, not unreasonably, invited the band to play *their* anthem. The Trumpeters had never heard it. But after an exchange of nervous glances they blew a few bold notes. The Mexicans were visibly unmoved. The

THE STORY OF A JAZZ MAVERICK 47

musicians' mortification increased. One by one they stopped playing. Then everyone sat down in silence.

The band's days in Mexico were severely numbered after that and although it made a film short, presumably for some newsreel feature, there is no record that it was ever displayed.

Before leaving, Jack, inevitably, became involved with an admirer, a highly emotional Mexican girl. Due to some linguistic confusion and Jack's ease of consent she had become convinced that he intended to take her back to the States with him. When he reached the station she was already there with her suitcases. Realizing that any attempt to explain would compound the confusion, and with the train about to leave, Jack retreated to the rear, crossed the track and boarded from the other side through an open window. And as the train carried him out of Mexico, the South's Greatest Trombone Wonder suppressed a pang of guilt with the modest belief that within a week the girl would have completely forgotten him.

The Southern Trumpeters disbanded but shortly afterwards R. J. Marin joined forces with a saxophonist named John Youngberg and launched a new organization. This included George Hill, L. C. Duncan (saxophone and clarinet), Rand Sherfey (banjo), Eddie Koontz (trumpet) and Bob Turley (drums). It was soon enlivened by Shand and Teagarden, and in September 1925 contributed to the ballyhoo which attended the opening of the Peabody Hotel, Memphis.

'The Youngberg-Marin Peacocks,' said a local newspaper, 'are ten dapper fellows, all accomplished musicians, playing twenty-five different instruments.' Jack was credited with a mastery of three: trombone, euphonium and saw. Many years later George Hill spoke highly, in retrospect, of Teagarden's skill with the saw. Jack's memory, however, has remained strikingly weak on this phase of his career.

The Peacocks broadcast frequently on the Midnight Frolic Show over WMC, the *Commercial Appeal* radio station. The following item from the *Appeal* gives an indication of how dependent these radio bands were upon listeners' requests. 'Tonight they will start their programme with a medley air.

The entire list of numbers has not yet been selected but among those which will probably be played are *Waters of Minnetonka* and *Mexican Moon*. By the time these pieces are played it is hoped that there will be enough requests made to carry on through the hour. . . .'

This particular broadcast held an extra thrill. Next day the *Appeal* said, 'For a time flashes of lightning gave a sinister outlook to the programme and the station had to shut down for a few minutes for protection. During the intermission the boys got feeling good so that when they went back on the air they furnished a treat to jazz enthusiasts.'

Quite what the boys did during the intermission is not detailed.

Before he rejoined Doc Ross, the following year found Jack on a two weeks' job in the Somerset Club, a flashy San Antonio roadhouse. The band was advertised as the New Orleans Rhythm Masters. It is worthy of note because apart from Jack, Shand and the Mexican drummer Amos Ayala it included two genuine links with the early New Orleans days. Sydney Arodin (clarinet) and the saxophonist Charlie Cordilla. Cordilla, in fact, accompanied the fabled 'Stale Bread' Lacoume in various sidewalk spasm bands during the very early nineteen-hundreds.

Teagarden rejoined Ross to tour the west coast. The band's entry into Los Angeles was supervised by Solomon, of Solomon's Penny Dance Deluxe, a downtown establishment known to be popular with the waterfront crowd. Little wonder, for in exchange for the admission fee of one cent, customers were not only offered a choice of brightly painted hostesses to dance with but were entertained by two bands, King Porter's and a sweet-playing group known as the Gutterson Orchestra. Solomon was now to add a third which he heralded as Ranger Ross and his Cowboys. They came from Texas, didn't they?

Solomon nourished Barnum-like ambitions and had already promoted a series of dance marathons. Upon the musicians' arrival he hustled them over to Santa Monica where he dressed them in the gaudiest cowboy outfits he could rent. Then he ordered them to climb aboard a locomotive he had chartered.

This was accomplished with some effort and a few sulphurous remarks directed at Solomon. Jack, however, was in that seventh heaven known only to small boys and amateur engineers. He perched himself on the cowcatcher, crimson chaps flapping, and vaguely fancied himself in some tableau of the railroad pioneer days, playing a role he couldn't quite specify. It was an exciting vision, heightened as the locomotive charged forward, and marred only by the cumbersome incongruity of his trombone.

At the station they were met by an enthusiastic crowd and a detachment of mounted policemen. With a true showman's brashness Solomon hauled the officers off their steeds and ordered the Cowboys to mount. There began a confused struggle involving horses, men and instruments. Jack, who had never been closer to a horse than to place a two-dollar bet, found himself astride the animal with his trombone entangled in the harness.

The horses trotted placidly enough until the procession reached 5th and Maine where the over-elated Solomon insisted they form a circle and strike up the band. Gingerly, the musicians raised their instruments. They began *California, Here I Come*. At the first wavering blast each of the nine horses reared. Teagarden dropped his horn and flung his arms about the animal's neck. Several of the cowboys slid ignominiously to the ground and bit the dust just like the Indians were doing weekly in the movie serials. The crowd appreciated this and hooted loudly.

Ranger Ross's men reformed on foot and marched the rest of the way to the Dance Deluxe. Here they began a tenure frequently interrupted by dance-floor fist fights which the patrons, turning their backs to the musicians, watched eagerly. Under these conditions it was impossible for the Ranger Ross Texas Cowboys to maintain their customary cheerfulness. But they would continue playing, albeit with a lack of heat, until the Gutterson Orchestra, with sickly smiles and syrupy melodies, came on to relieve them.

The following summer found the Doc Ross band in New

Mexico. One hot afternoon in Alberquerque the door of Jack's
hotel room opened to admit a jug-jawed stranger carrying a
trumpet case and a collie dog. Jack was sleeping. He hadn't
long gone to bed.

The man with the dog wore a demoniacal grin. He widened
it a further inch, thrust his face and the dog's close to the sleeper
and shook him awake. Teagarden blinked his eyes open. He
rolled away so sharply he almost fell off the bed.

'Hi,' said the stranger huskily. 'I'm Wingy Mannone.' He
placed the dog on Teagarden's pillow. 'And this is Bebe.'

Wingy and Bebe joined the Ross band for a season at the Del
Norte Hotel, El Paso. On the way there, Jack who was driving
noted that the cigarette in Wingy's hand was burning danger-
ously close to his fingers. Nervously, he sniffed the scent of
charred wood. He was unaware of Wingy's artificial limb until
that moment. The shock all but drove him off the road. Wingy,
of course, was convulsed all the way to El Paso.

At the Del Norte, Jack was joined by Ora, Jack Jr. and their
new baby Gilbert. At once Wingy demonstrated his one-armed
proficiency by changing Gilbert's diapers in less time than it
took the parents. Only Bebe the dog was unimpressed. Bebe
had attended all of Wingy's escapades and was conditioned to
be surprised by none. She even watched without interest while
master and Teagarden dug a hole one day in the middle of the
mesa and buried, for eternal preservation, a copy of Louis
Armstrong's *Oriental Strut.*

Wingy's presence in the Doc Ross unit was cut short following a card game with Ross. A dispute arose, epithets were
exchanged and Wingy packed his horn, picked up Bebe, and
departed.

Most of Teagarden's touring through the south-west was done
in a reliable Ford sedan. He felt not too happy with it for it
afforded few opportunities for mechanical tinkering. He was
on the lookout for a more challenging machine and found one
in a Houston parking lot. It was a Stanley Steamer in an
advanced state of rust and clearly ostracized by the other
vehicles. He inquired of the lot proprietor who told him it had

belonged to a whiskey runner (now lodging in Houston jail) and nobody knew how to operate it.

'You can have it,' said the man, 'for the hundred and twenty-five dollars storage charge.'

Jack borrowed the money from Doc Ross and closed the deal. That Stanley Steamer became a familiar, if somewhat fearsome, sight along the highways of the old south-west. Sometimes it conveyed the whole Teagarden family. In fact, Jack Jr. appeared in it so often that the Doc Ross men nicknamed him Steamer.

When Jack tired of the Stanley he drove it to Oklahoma City and left it with his brother Charles to sell. Some time later he got a letter. Charles had placed an advertisement in the newspaper. Two men answered it. They requested a demonstration drive, took off without Charles and were never seen again.

Doc Ross wound up the summer of 1927 with a profitable six weeks' stint at the Gunther Hotel, San Antonio. Then the season trailed off with a scattering of one-nighters. The boys found themselves with time on their hands. They became even more changeable, impulsive. One day in late September somebody said, 'Let's drive to California.' Teagarden agreed at once; but a week later he sat in a Cadillac tourer heading north for New York. Snaps Elliot had received word that work was awaiting him up there, and had taken off immediately. His wife was to follow in their Cadillac.

'It's too big a trip for a girl to tackle alone,' murmured Teagarden.

Red Hawn, a banjo player, agreed. 'I hear everything's happening in New York,' he said. He'd been all set for California.

They bundled their instruments and luggage in the Cadillac and set off. The journey was uneventful until they ran into a police ambush outside Xenia, Ohio, and were charged for speeding. They were hauled before a sleepy J.P. who eyed them with distaste and fined them mercilessly.

It was a mild evening when they reached New York. Red Hawn was driving. Jack fell asleep in the middle of Lincoln Tunnel and Mrs. Elliot woke him up in the middle of Times

Square. Full of wonder they drove up and down Broadway at least eight times. Then Mrs. Elliot left to join her husband. Hawn and Jack found a phone booth.

'Let's call Red Nichols,' said Hawn.

They did and got no answer.

'Try Miff Mole,' said Teagarden. Again no answer. He shrugged. After all, Mole and Nichols were the busiest, biggest jazz names in New York. But all of a sudden the roaring city surrounding the phone booth seemed a town of no answer. Teagarden waited for the brief homesick twinge to pass. Then he called another number.

This time he got through and announced himself. From the other end came a stream of gleeful obscenity, hoarsely voiced. Jack hung up. 'Wingy wants us to come right over,' he said.

They stepped out of the phone booth. There was a glow in the sky over Broadway. The sounds of Manhattan were a friendly all-in chorus.

Chapter VI

JACK TEAGARDEN'S first New York residence was the Marie Antoinette Hotel. As he checked in, New Yorkers were talking about Babe Ruth's sixtieth home run and the latest attack on the underworld's favourite clay pigeon, Jack Diamond. It was 1927 and the ballyhoo era still had two years of life, but it had reached its climax a few months earlier with the city's fantastic welcome to Lindbergh. Since then, other transatlantic fliers had taken the famous noon ride up Broadway. Golf champions too, channel swimmers, foreign politicians and Italian soccer players. But the ticker-tape blizzards were slackening. Flagpole sitters and marathon dancers persisted but watchers no longer gaped. They scoffed instead, then turned to a more intriguing novelty when the Warners added sound to *The Jazz Singer*.

The talkies came as one blow to New York's cabarets. Another fell when the law carted Texas Guinan off to jail for repeated prohibition violations and snatched the piano from under Helen Morgan in her 54th Street club. The cabarets were already getting stiff competition from the flourishing dance halls where tango teas were replacing the Charleston.

And, of course, cabarets could not supply illicit liquor with the discretion or facility of the speakeasies. Nor was the quality of the brew so good in the large Broadway establishments as in the smaller side-street joints whose number was legion. Probably the heaviest concentration of speakeasies in America

would have been found in the clamorous light-splashed rect-
angle bordered by 40th and 59th Streets, and 5th and 9th
Avenues. Federal men estimated that 45th Street was the
wettest in the nation.

Despite the prowling of undercover police 'Sheik and Sheba'
squads, employed to check on the behaviour of gigolos and
dance hostesses, many of the speaks were strategically located
near the dance halls. Thus not only were the patrons able to
refresh themselves for the dances. It was that much easier for
the musicians to slip out during intermission. The convenience
was particularly appreciated by bandsmen forced to suppress
strong jazz urges.

For the dance hall and hotel orchestras of Manhattan were
thoroughly influenced by Paul Whiteman's symphonic jazz
style. The barnstorming vigour of the south-west, so familiar
to Teagarden, was nowhere to be found. Instead, he encountered a pattern of grimly sentimental melodies framed within
heavy ornate arrangements. The pattern was, on rare occasions,
disturbed by solo explosions of considerable heat from the more
gifted and irrepressible jazz players. But opportunity for sustained improvisation was absent in such fashionable organizations as Al Lynn's, Pancho's, Oliver Naylor's, Leo Reisman's,
and Paul Specht's. Consequently, many musicians sought relief
in private assemblies. Dominant among these were Loring 'Red'
Nichols, who played a cornet and Milfred 'Miff' Mole the
trombonist. This skilful pair, themselves occasionally refugees
from the large orchestras, led their following into the recording
studios. The purpose continued to be self-enjoyment rather than
monetary gain. These young men, after all, represented the best
dance music talent in New York at the time, and were assured
of substantial earnings from employment with the 'grind' bands.

Although unfettered by ponderous arrangements, this 'after
hours' music was clearly disciplined. It was, in fact, a direct but
elegant offspring of the Original Dixieland Jazz Band, the white
unit from New Orleans which had hit Reisenweber's Café in
1917, delivered an historically raucous punch and soon thereafter knocked itself out of existence.

The Mole-Nichols recording groups consisted of assorted personnels under a variety of pseudonyms—Red Heads, Five Pennies, Little Molars, Arkansas Travellers, etc. While they ruled the field of escape from big band orthodoxy in New York, there were a few kindred movements. One, an offshoot of Paul Specht's Orchestra, was called the Georgians. Another, the Scranton Sirens, featured two sons of a Pennsylvania coal-field bandmaster named Dorsey.

The recording output of this school was enormous but no musical revolution occurred. The goal of each studio session was liberty rather than experiment, a brief slackening of inhibitions imposed by the strait-jacket formality of the swank orchestras. Yet, they were in effect proving-grounds for young men of talent.

In 1927 Mole's playing was far in advance of any white recording trombonist. His command of the instrument was so supple as to make others sound fumbling. Hitherto, the trombone in jazz had been employed chiefly for smears, swoops and chord bases. Few, if any, jazz trombonists ventured to explore the instrument's possibilities for melodic improvisation. Mole proved once and for all that the trombone and flexibility were not irreconcilable.

Miff Mole is one example of the growth in individual skills which, while praiseworthy, formed the only progress of the white New Yorkers. Their style was still basically that of the Dixielanders of ten years earlier. Few of the Red Nichols groups advanced much beyond it. But its days were numbered. By mid-1928 several young men from Chicago were bringing into town a manner hotly eloquent of the dynamic influence they had absorbed from the New Orleans Negroes who had followed the Mississippi north.

The Chicagoans displayed qualities unknown to the white New Yorkers. Earthiness instead of elegance, power rather than polish. This was not, however, what the society band leaders wanted and at first a hard struggle confronted the youths from the Windy City. But they soon merged with local personnel for recording dates which their style, being the lustier, dominated. And the piles of pre-1929 Nichols-Mole records became what Wilder Hobson has called the final development or last stand of the 'white' manner of jazz playing.

If the advent of the Chicagoans upset the Nichols-Mole monopoly on white jazz, that of Jack Teagarden removed Miff's supremacy on the trombone. Not that there was any question of challenge and overthrow. Teagarden's respect for Mole was considerable. But the rough agility of the Texan's delivery, the strong emotional content of his tone more completely reflected the elemental spirit of jazz than did that of any other white musician. This did not invite instant commercial success (since undiluted jazz was not a popular commodity) but it delighted the vigorous Chicagoans and his admittance to their brotherhood was inevitable.

But not immediate. Teagarden's first New York job was a short-lived stint with Wingy Mannone in Brooklyn. Mannone did not discover Teagarden as has sometimes been stated. He has other claims to fame—his 'jive' lexicography, the naming of 52nd Street 'Swing Alley', the joke which allegedly caused a Los Angeles zoot-suit riot, and an undisputed authority on chicken cacciatore. But his unofficial press-agentry on Teagarden's behalf in the fall of 1927 undoubtedly brought the Texan's name before many New Yorkers who had never heard of him.

From Brooklyn, Teagarden's trombone took him to Broadway and the glittering sweat shop called Roseland. Hip flask toters, Charleston marathons, tired and short-skirted 'dime-a-dance' girls ('200 beautiful hostesses'—but the Depression cut the fee to a cent), all the fevered symptoms of the era's hedonism were on display inside the walk-up ballroom at 51st and Broadway. In jazz annals, however, the name of Roseland at once brings to mind Henderson.

While the large Manhattan society bands were pouring out their ornate trivia and the Nichols-Mole escapists fled regularly to the recording studios, a quite different situation existed in Harlem. Here, well organized bands, small groups and solo acts were flourishing in the Negro resorts. Their spirited performances excited the local populace and genuinely intrigued many white visitors. It also, sometimes self-consciously, attracted

The publicity postcard for the 1924 Mexican concerts

Jack operating a Mexican street car

Jack with bandleader R. J. Marin on a pyramid in Mexico

those white society elements who liked to be classed as sophisticated and who considered it daringly fashionable to enter
Harlem and witness what they hoped were unbridled exhibitions
of Negro song and dance. The resultant boom brought prosperity to many Harlem entertainers but no licence to extend
their talents beyond the district's limits. The Negro musicians
had few bridgeheads in white territory. One was established by
Fletcher Henderson in the Roseland in 1922.

Henderson was a man of easy disposition and high talent for
arrangement and organization. Arriving in New York City from
Georgia just after the First World War he formed a large dance
band which served as a regular house band at the Roseland for
most of the next two decades. It was the first and for many
years the only coloured orchestra in New York operating outside Harlem. Under Henderson's direction at one time or
another worked the finest Negro jazz musicians of all time.

Roseland also employed a white band to alternate with the
Henderson group. It served not only to provide relief for the
house unit but also to furnish a change of pace for breathless
patrons. Billy Lustig's band was discharging this task when
Teagarden joined it.

Until he heard Henderson's men in action Jack was unaware
of the affinity his musical style bore to that of the best Negro
players. He was particularly startled by the playing of Jimmy
Harrison, one of Henderson's outstanding trombonists, for it
contained those same qualities of feeling which had animated
Jack's playing ever since his childhood. Much of the phrasing
and tone produced by the two men was similar if not identical.
Neither was dismayed by the coincidence and they had little
time for the later conjectures of critics seeking evidence of
influence. Whatever they held in common was related to feelings and modes of expression innate to each musician long
before they met.

Neither did it spark any rivalry. Instead they became good
friends. Jack was a frequent guest at Harrison's home which
he shared with drummer Kaiser Marshall. Harrison drank little
but feasted on banquets of ice cream, cake, baked spareribs,

chitterlings and sweet potatoes. Sometimes they moved to
Coleman Hawkins' home near by where, with the tenor saxophone ace playing piano for a change, the quartet would get
down to some serious jamming.

From the moment they met, Hawkins was to testify years
later, it was impossible to separate Teagarden and Harrison.
They listened to each other raptly, kidded each other and drew
forth each other's professional admiration. Both knew they were
different from other trombonists, but neither had the time or
the sense of perspective to realize that separately, yet almost
simultaneously, they had liberated the trombone from barnyard
glissandi, martial 'oompah' and other comic or special effects.
This in no way slights the talented and highly individualist
practitioners in these forms. If, by the late 'twenties, Kid Ory's
broad undulations were beginning to sound leaden and old
fashioned, exciting properties certainly dwelled in the aggressive
smears of Charlie Irvis and the imaginative mute work of Joe
Nanton—while Harrison's fellow trombonist on the Henderson
roster, Charlie 'Big' Green will always be remembered as the
possessor of a sardonic slurring which found its ideal in the
accompaniments to some of Bessie Smith's more cynical blues
commentaries. These men, all Negro, were doing things with
the trombone that could hardly have been conceived of in the
instrument's history. But in direct and serious employment of
it for the simple expression of jazz feeling and melodic creation,
shorn of all trimmings and special effects, Harrison had appeared
to be both peerless and a pioneer. Thus it is not difficult
to visualize his surprise and, such was his nature, pleasure
at meeting a *white* who was doing precisely the same thing.

Added to his musical prowess Harrison possessed a flair for
'down-South preacher' impersonations. His act was featured at
the Roseland while the band played appropriate camp-meeting
music behind him. He always had a ready laugh even when
racked with the pains of his stomach ulcers. These finally
defeated him and he died in Wiley Private Sanatorium aged
thirty-one.

One night at the Roseland, Henderson stopped Jack as the

Lustig players were leaving the stand. The band leader said, 'I have been listening to you. I don't see how any white man can play like you do.' His voice lowered. 'Tell me—and you have my strictest confidence—are you coloured?'

Flattered and embarrassed, Jack shook his head.

Henderson half-smiled. 'You can tell me, you know. I wouldn't say a word.' He walked away, doubt still curving the smile on his lips. That doubt, Jack suspected, lingered beyond their Roseland acquaintance although the matter was never brought up again.

The pattern was now dance hall to speakeasy to bed to dance hall. It was not always the same bed. The Manhattan jazz musician moved within a shifting circle of familiarity. He dropped into a friend's hotel room, went on to work from there, met afterwards in an off-Broadway cellar, left there for someone else's place where an informal music session was already kicking. If at any moment during his sunset to noon itinerary he were stopped and asked his rightful address he might pause and very likely give a wrong one. His habitat was Broadway, and its dark branches. Otherwise he was of no fixed abode. Teagarden was to comment on this during one of the most spirited blues sessions ever recorded:

> I can't figure out how these Broadway sports ever get
>   their sleep.
> They walk the streets all night like a policeman on his
>   beat.

But inevitably the footloose sport would drift into a dependable little harbour on West 53rd Street, four doors off Broadway, beneath the shadow of the crosstown El and across the street from the Arcadia Ballroom. Jimmy Plunkett's, of hallowed memory to almost every prominent jazz man, was more than just a hangout for thirsty musicians. It was an information booth where bar-rail chatter revealed the names of arrivals, departures and availables in the Manhattan music world. It was an employment agency where radio and recording executive met horn-toting hopefuls, where trumpets were unsheathed and auditions often conducted on the spot. Sometimes entire bands were organized at the bar.

Occasionally business transactions spilled over into a small back room, where differences of opinion were also settled but rarely with violence. It served too as changing-room for any musician who had just signed an unexpected contract and whose services were required immediately. He might have no tux with him, but there was usually a spare one among the clothes and instruments scattered about the rear. Much of the time Plunkett's back room vaguely resembled the training quarters of some slovenly but musically-inclined prize fighter. In the midst of the clamour of hopes, deals, plans, agreements and discords, Jim Plunkett served liquor and encouragement with equal readiness. The customer who had just landed a record date or a hotel spot would buy the drinks for an unemployed companion. The uncertainties of the profession were such that their positions might be reversed next week. Both men knew it— Jimmy Plunkett knew it. So he rarely bothered about cash but kept a musicians' account book and served them drinks on the cuff. Some ran up bills of three and even four figures and it is doubtful if Plunkett was ever fully repaid—financially that is. But his was the unique pleasure of witnessing a bizarre parade of American life across the cement floor of his eighteen-foot speakeasy. Colourful figures and great musicians confided in him while they drank his liquor. Many of them are gone. Plunkett and the cap he always wore to hide his baldness are gone. Plunkett's Bar has vanished, and the premises are now a storeroom for the Palladium Dance Hall.

A February night in 1928 found Teagarden in the Brooklyn home of Billy Lustig helping celebrate the birth of a son to Mrs. Lustig. Most of the band was present along with a lively group of showgirls from the Club Monterey. They included Elaine Manzi, a popular toe dancer. Lustig selected a strikingly pretty brunette and presented her to Jack.

'Clare, here's a fine musician you've got to meet,' said Lustig. 'He's from Texas.'

She looked at Teagarden as if he were from the moon.

'You'll be her escort,' Lustig ordered.

More or less Jack remained her escort for the next eight years. Though Clare Manzi was Elaine's sister and possessed the good looks, vivacity and whatever other qualities the 1928 chorus line demanded, she was no showgirl. She was fully alive to the glamour of show business but its upheavals checked her from entering it. Possibly she was unaware that show business in its most unsettled form was manifest in the life of a wandering jazz musician. Her association with Jack would soon enlighten her.

Two weeks after their first meeting she and Lustig called on him. He was then living in a shabby room at Mansfield Hall. He wasn't at home so they waited in what passed for a lobby. When he appeared his face beamed with boyish excitement. He was carrying a phonograph record. After a brief greeting he ushered them over to a victrola and cranked it. Carefully he lowered the needle. A sprightly but undeviating arrangement of *I Just Roll Along* burst forth with banjo and cymbal supporting the whine of reeds and brass. The orchestra's fidelity to the melody was remarkable even for that day. Clearly it was no school for a jazz musician.

'Listen,' said Jack proudly, 'I'm in there somewhere.'

And he was. It was the first of over a thousand recordings. An enormous wealth of recorded musicianship would grow from that sugary, ricky-ticky *I Just Roll Along* spinning on the victrola in Mansfield Hall on a wintry afternoon in 1928. His solo was brief, lacking the brashness which was to come later, yet the technical ability and blueness somehow crept through. No subsequent recording would excite him more.

A few nights later an elongated shadow fell across the bed on which he was lying and a reproachful voice said, 'Been looking all over for you.' Teagarden opened his eyes. 'Pee Wee,' he said, and closed them again.

'Refresh yourself and let's go.' Pee Wee thrust a jug at him. 'Bring your horn. Better get your clothes on too,' he added thoughtfully.

While Teagarden dressed, Pee Wee finished the jug. Then they went out. The streets were freezing. Jack tugged his cap over his ears. The two men turned off Broadway into 51st Street, came to a speakeasy and entered.

Pee Wee pointed to a slender youth who was conducting a conversation with dramatic gestures. 'That's Bud Freeman,' said Pee Wee. The target of Freeman's oratory was a handsome, beefy blond boy whom Russell introduced as Jimmy McPartland.

'They're with Benny Pollack,' explained Pee Wee. The Pollack band was working at the Little Club, a lavish cellar under the 44th Street theatre. Cutting Freeman off in the middle of a particularly eloquent declamation Pee Wee announced, 'This is the trombonist I told you about. He's come all the way from Texas.'

'He looks it,' murmured McPartland.

'Play,' said Freeman theatrically.

Jack hesitated. Without a word someone pushed a drink at him. He swallowed it and unpacked his horn. By then a second drink had appeared and he knew he was among friends. The choruses he subsequently delivered were loosely based on *Diane*. They flowed out from the speak and warmed 51st Street over a distance of two blocks east and west.

Jack's solo impressed even Bud Freeman into silence. But not for long. He urged McPartland to his feet and they left to pluck other members of Pollack's band from the shady resorts to which they had adjourned when the Little Club closed. Then the whole mob swept up to the Louisiana Apartments on West 48th. Here, within soundproof rooms, dwelt Vic Berton, the young white drummer of the Red Nichols circle.

It was a general policy of hotel managers to keep musicians in rooms one above the other, instead of on the same floor. Thus the noise from their irregular habits and uninhibited rehearsals would disturb non-musical guests less than themselves. Complete insulation was, of course, impossible. Especially when there might be as many as six all-night jazz parties going on in a vertical series from street floor to roof. Daily the harassed hotel staffs were plagued with complaints from sleepless guests.

That Vic Berton enjoyed considerable popularity with the Louisiana Apartments staff was partly due to the generosity of his tipping. This also served to brace them against the protests which might result from any sudden breakdown in the sound-proofing of Berton's apartment.

When Teagarden arrived blankets were being hung over the windows as assistance to the soundproofing. The function started a trifle later than was customary—about 3.30 a.m. By dawn the place was crowded with some of the most illustrious figures in white jazz history. They were there, of course, without a notion of future fame or vicissitude. More immediate matters were the hardness of the floor (seating accommodation having proved inadequate), how to let the suffocating smoke out, who'll take the next chorus and where the hell's my gin?

Vic Berton rapped his cymbal briskly. Jimmy McPartland pointed a trumpet at the single blue light bulb in the ceiling socket and at his elbow, Freeman muttered ferociously through his tenor sax. Pee Wee Russell grimaced approvingly at the pungent phrasings of another clarinet player, a teenager named Benny Goodman, while Vic Breidis, pale and bespectacled, nodded joyfully at the piano, his dark fate as a suicide mercifully hidden from him. In the centre of the room directly under the blue glow and perched on an upended orange-crate, Jack closed his eyes and led the assembly in a warm attack on the blues. A few feet from him Pollack's trombonist Glenn Miller rested his horn and bowed graciously to a master.

With that Louisiana Apartments gathering, Teagarden made his primary impact upon the New York jazz scene. A few mornings later he was sleeping off another heavy night in Pee Wee's refuge at the bottom of Mansfield Hall. The bodies of other temporarily displaced musicians littered the floor. The phone rang and Pee Wee groped for it.

'Vic Berton,' the voice said. 'I need that trombonist Beergarden . . . or was it Teabottom? The guy you fetched to my place the other night.'

Pee Wee looked at the floor. He prodded Jack with his foot. 'I think I can find him. Where you at?'

'Victor studios. With Wolfe Kahn. Miff Mole hasn't shown up. We're set to record in an hour.'

Pee Wee kicked Teagarden, harder this time. 'I'll look around. Say, Vic,' he lowered his voice nervously, 'you need a clarinet too?'

Berton hung up.

By now Jack was stirring. Pee Wee primed him with a stew of week-old coffee grounds. Half an hour later Berton picked him up in a cab.

Along Broadway Roger Wolfe Kahn was considered a wonder boy. His millionaire family was renowned for its patronage of opera and similar high arts. Roger had shattered the tradition by organizing several jazz bands and composing such stomp tunes as *Crazy Rhythm*. The Kahn clan had dismissed him as a problem child only to readmit him with awe when he disclosed earnings amounting to twice those of President Harding. Kahn was just eighteen.

Despite his youth, Roger Wolfe Kahn was well hardened to the habits of jazz musicians. None the less he winced when Teagarden staggered into the studio. There were short introductions. Jack met the pianist, Art Schutt, guitarist, Eddie Lang and Joe Venuti, the violinist. Then he turned to the microphone. It greeted him with an open leer and he shrank from it. But under the hammer blows of Pee Wee's coffee his hangover began to fade. The mike became impersonal and the steady beat of Eddie Lang's guitar kept him upright.

It was, Kahn said years later, a miracle. The trombonist had arrived at ten in the morning unquestionably wearing the largest hangover on Manhattan Island. Like a veteran he played every note of the whole arrangement blending with the brass section as if it wasn't the first time he'd heard it. To crown everything he blew a smoothly delightful *ad lib* chorus which, although fleeting, rescued *She's a Great Great Girl* from the oblivion to which thousands of contemporary 'popular' offerings were speedily consigned.

By the end of spring Teagarden's invigorating presence was heard on several 'dime store' records. His solos were brief and usually limited to one per side. Each was a buoyant, even startling interruption of the generally turgid band score. It gave the performance a quality of the unexpected. It turned many a mediocre record into a future collector's item.

But income from recording dates was neither sizeable nor steady. Jack was forced to cut down personal expenses. He left Mansfield Hall and found cheaper accommodation in a West Side rooming house of depressing aspect. He was further discouraged when a tempting offer from Philadelphia proved worthless. He made the trip with Chummy McGregor, a pianist. They drove back to New York in a morose temper which wasn't improved when they got lost near the Holland Tunnel and caused a chaotic traffic jam as Chummy, who stammered badly under stress, sought directions from a policeman similarly afflicted.

Next morning a dark dapper man entered Jack's room and offered him a job. Teagarden was in no mood to consider fabulous job offers and suppressed an urge to throw a shoe at him. But he listened with unconcealed scepticism.

'As you wish,' finished the newcomer, 'but if you change your mind call me at the Manger Hotel. Remember, the name's Pollack.'

The Ben Pollack orchestra was to develop into one of the most interesting aggregations in jazz history. Already it included several highly talented individualists who obeyed their improvisational impulses as often as possible. Despite this, the band enjoyed commercial popularity. Pollack himself was an unexciting but hard-driving drummer who had once sparked the New Orleans Rhythm Kings, probably the best of the early white jazz bands. In 1924 Pollack formed his own band, opened at the Venice Ballroom in Los Angeles and a year later was joined by Benny Goodman, then aged sixteen. Gil Rodin and Glenn Miller wrote most of the band's orchestrations; and although the group played its share of waltzes and sentimental foxtrots, it occasionally captured a romping verve hitherto the trademark of small groups. In the words of Rodin's later claim, 'Pollack's was the first white band playing hot in New York City.'

Studied orchestrations gave it a polish and, although violins were added for ballroom effect, jazz heat was rarely far from the surface. And why not? The band's nucleus contained two fine saxophone players in Larry Binyon and Gil Rodin, as well as the sturdy Chicagoans Jimmy McPartland, and Benny and Harry Goodman.

These all felt that Teagarden's presence in the band would improve its vitality. It is probable that the incumbent trombonist Glenn Miller shared their view. In no way does this reflect upon Miller as a musician. It was simply that Teagarden's approach to the spirit of jazz was identical with the Chicago members of Pollack's band at least. So that when Miller bowed out of the band, citing as a reason his reluctance to continue on the road, Teagarden moved in.

The job had a little more class than any other he had previously worked at and presented an initial problem. He enlisted the aid of Ray Bauduc with whom he had formed a strong friendship. Ray was playing drums in a 51st Street crypt known as the Playground.

'Ray,' said Jack, 'I join Pollack on Monday. I need a double-breasted vest and striped pants.'

They went over to Bauduc's apartment which he shared with Jimmy Dorsey. Bauduc dug out a vest. 'Here,' he said.

'How about striped pants?'

'I can't help you.' Ray hesitated, then rummaged around a bit more. 'Try these,' he said, 'they're Jimmy Dorsey's.'

'Where's Jimmy?'

'In Europe,' replied Bauduc.

Teagarden returned the trousers later and Bauduc replaced them in his trunk. When Jimmy got back he couldn't get the trunk open. Ray had the key. Where was Ray? In Europe. They had, in fact, passed each other in mid-ocean.

The Pollack band was out on an eastern tour and early in July 1928 moved into the Million Dollar Pier, Atlantic City. Shortly afterwards, Jack joined and quickly established popularity with his colleagues. At first, however, he was disconcerted by the clarinettist Benny Goodman. Each time Jack stood up to take a solo he was conscious of Benny's frowning scrutiny. This went on for weeks until Teagarden, puzzled and resentful, drew Goodman aside in the dressing-room and asked for an explanation.

'I like to watch you when you play, that's all,' said Benny.

'Then why the frown?'

'What frown?' Benny was bewildered. Further discussion revealed that the frown was actually a squint caused by Benny's shy disinclination to wear glasses on the stand. Thereafter, his narrow-eyed study failed to disturb the boldness of Teagarden's solos.

Goodman used a clarinet style somewhat different from that which the world was to hear a decade hence. If in 1938 his adopted kinship was with Reginald Kell, in 1928 his natural affinity was to Pee Wee Russell. He was not as raw, as intense, as Russell. But his tone often expressed the same husky warmth.

Neither Goodman nor Teagarden were leaders in the escapades of Pollack's boys. But they enjoyed a healthy share of the fun. The whole band clowned freely, particularly because it had a couple of natural pranksters in Benny's bass playing brother, Harry, and Dick 'Icky' Morgan, the banjoist.

It was Morgan who originated an 'Icky' language which the boys would employ to baffle any eavesdropping stranger. His intrusion would be signalled by the words, 'Nix crackin', Jimmy Bracken.' From that moment the conversation would be continued in a jargon quite unintelligible to the newcomer and frequently to the speakers themselves.

Dick Morgan was also featured in 'Boop-a-Doop' comedy vocals but perhaps his most memorable attempt was to discourage Ben Pollack's urge to sing. It happened shortly after Ray Bauduc had joined the band as a drummer. Pollack, released from the drums, was now able to conduct his men as he felt a bandleader should. Then Bernie Foyer took over as band manager. He conceived ideas which, if practised, would have turned the band into a vaudeville act. Some were and did. But when Foyer persuaded Pollack that he might be a second Rudy

Vallee, they suspected he was going too far. They were sure when they heard Pollack sing.

He sang through a megaphone in the then popular Vallee fashion. One night the band played the introductory chords, Pollack beamed, waved the megaphone and pressed it to his lips. He broke into *I'm a Ding Dong Daddy from Dumas*. His smile vanished. He spluttered. Behind him the band romped through its well-rehearsed accompaniment with difficulty. Some of its members were convulsed. They included Dick Morgan who might have been seen earlier smearing limburger cheese over the mouthpiece.

Undismayed, Pollack not only sang a number of popular songs but 'signed' several recordings with a feeble 'May it please you, Benny Pollack'. This bit of unnecessary politeness planted an anti-climax on the record and the need of a stiff drink in Jack each time he heard it.

When the band played *Tiger Rag*, Harry Goodman donned a tiger head. It had no noticeable effect on his bass playing. For *St. James Infirmary* the lights were dimmed and Jack preached chorus after chorus on the trombone while Ray strutted across the stage dressed as an undertaker. Sometimes, when Ray was involved in this routine, Pollack took to the drums. Upon occasion he would venture to them even as Bauduc played and absently tap the cymbals with his baton. Bauduc's reaction to this habit can be imagined.

After Atlantic City the band played four weeks at the Oakmont, Pittsburgh, then dissolved for a layoff. Pollack went home to Chicago. Rodin hung around New York on the lookout for bookings. N.B.C. was controlling the band and arranged an audition at the Park Central Hotel. Rodin wired Pollack immediately. Pollack was just unpacking. He repacked in a hurry and returned to New York. So did his musicians. They were in varying degrees of fitness for the try-out but the hotel manager liked them. 'The job's yours,' he told Pollack, 'if you'll add two fiddles and a 'cello.'

The added string section consisted of Eddie Bergman, Al Beller and Bill Schumann. Schumann, the 'cellist, was also an avid stock market speculator who more than once skipped rehearsals to double on Wall Street. One night he grasped his 'cello after Beller and Bergman had been tampering with it. He began to play and it collapsed. Some months later, Wall Street, Schumann's other interest, collapsed too.

The band opened at the Park Central in late September playing from the balcony in the Florentine Grill where the customers were rather more sophisticated than those Jack Teagarden had been accustomed to blowing for. Week-end nights were enlivened by visits from the college set. But everybody seemed congenial and brought his own bottled refreshments. Prohibition was the great leveller.

Recordings and outside work were netting Teagarden a salary of about $250 a week. Getting rid of it was no problem. If you couldn't lose it within a half-mile radius of the Park Central, there was always Harlem. According to contemporary police estimates, Harlem contained eleven 'white trade' nightclubs (they included the Cotton Club, Connie's Inn, Small's Paradise and the Saratoga) and five hundred 'lower rank cabarets'. Five out of seven cigar stores and lunch-rooms, the statistics continue, were speakeasies. Unnumbered were such establishments as buffet flats, whist clubs, Democrat headquarters and other two-bits-a-drink joints.

Bauduc, the Goodmans, McPartland, Dick Morgan and other young white musicians made the up-town pilgrimage often enough. With Jack it was almost a nightly ritual. 'Seems like you make every rent party,' Coleman Hawkins told him one 3 a.m. in Pod's and Jerry's, a one-room speak between 7th and Lennox. Though in its original form a rent party was a highly practical function, it had become a term of general application to any Harlem function where two or more musicians were gathered together.

The Pollack boys would go straight from work at the Park Central picking up wives or girl friends *en route*. The first stop might be Small's Paradise to hear Charlie Johnson's band and Willie Jackson perform *Golf Playin' Papa*, a monologue spiced with *ad lib* obscenities, or Connie's Inn to hear Louis Armstrong

heading the *Hot Chocolates* revue. In each place the white boys
were treated royally and invariably given the best tables. The
Negro musicians acknowledged the true purpose of their visits.
They knew that many of these youngsters had haunted similar
establishments on the South Side of Chicago. Then, as now,
the reason was the same. They felt at home with this music
and therefore with the musicians. The Negroes repaid the
compliment by keeping a watchful eye on those of their young
visitors who, when feeling too much at home, became targets
for the local larcenists.

When the big spots closed, the boys and their girls went on to
Pod's and Jerry's. This resort contained a few tables, unlimited
fried chicken, gin and a piano. The gin was sometimes blended
with a little wine to form Top and Bottom. This concoction was
pink, tasted not unlike perfume and sold for 35 cents a pint. The
piano deserves immortality in a museum. At one time or other
it was played by the most distinguished Negro jazz pianists.
Among these was the mighty World War I veteran Willie the
Lion Smith. Battered hat tipped over one eye, cigar jutting
upwards to meet it, the Lion hotly harangued the piano while he
played. Now caressing it with hoarse endearments, now roaring
abuse at it, he would produce a rolling stream of exciting patterns.

Fats Waller, whose jubilation seemed to increase with every
alimony crisis which confronted him, was another frequent
visitor. So was his teacher, James P. Johnson. One morning
before dawn, Fats, James P. and the Lion in turn attacked the
piano for dozens of choruses of *Liza*. Then a fourth pianist
wandered in, a quiet young Negro known only as Beetle. It
seemed to Jack that his improvisations crowned them all. And
the next night he followed Beetle to his place of work, a gloomy
cellar lighted by one red bulb, but thereafter lost track of him.

The passage of time spins a web of fable about these Harlem
piano giants. But it is still recalled by those who were privileged
to know them that they reached the height of their creativity
when they played the blues. It was at such moments that
Teagarden was most moved to play with them. And, as if
reflective of the philosophy that sorrow should be resisted while

suffered, the mood of their playing was one of defiance as often as pathos.

When the blues gave way to wilder stomps, Jack, given enough Top and Bottom, would swoop Clare into his arms and execute a mock shimmy in the centre of the floor. Convinced it was the funniest thing in the world he would finish the dance helpless with laughter. His gaiety and the prevailing joyous spirit were sufficient to buoy Clare's strength against the onsets of fatigue. Never a physically sturdy girl, it is a tribute to her fortitude that she refused the stimulant of liquor. Her abstinence survived a way of life which often seemed submerged beneath a ceaseless flow of gin from bottle, barrel or bathtub. Sunrise would see Jack trailing happily along the Harlem sidewalks behind Clare, one big hand resting on her shoulder. And they would stop in at a rib joint for a breakfast of fried ribs before continuing downtown to reach home about noon. A record date would further postpone any rest until late in the afternoon.

One appointment in the fall of 1928 put Jack in good solid Chicago company. He and Jimmy McPartland joined Joe Sullivan (piano), Mezz Mezzrow (clarinet) and Eddie Condon (guitar) to cut a couple of numbers at the Okeh studios. The three Chicagoans were engaged in a sometimes desperate scramble for livelihood. Teagarden expressed their plight and attitude with the words:

> I'd rather drink muddy water Lord, sleep in a hollow
>   log,
> Than be up here in New York, treated like a dirty
>   dog. . . .

The second recording was a gayer piece entitled *I'm Sorry I Made You Cry*. It is notable for Artie Miller's grunting bass fiddle and an unbelievable vocal which Eddie Condon has never recalled without blushing.

In early November the Park Central received an unexpected stroke of publicity. It was half past ten on a Saturday night. A gambler named Arnold Rothstein staggered from his room on the third floor clutching his abdomen. He crawled down the servants' stairway to the lobby, collapsed and died from gunshot wounds. His killer was never found. Meanwhile, from the balcony of the Florentine Grill, Ben Pollack's orchestra was entertaining the customers with such tunes as *Freshman Hop, Sentimental Baby* and *She's One Sweet Show Girl.* For this selection some of the boys led by Ray Bauduc assembled in front of the band and swayed gently in what they hoped was Hawaiian hula fashion. They held straw fans which they waggled teasingly before their own, and occasionally each other's, bodies. This languid and inexpert routine was in no way related to the crime then being committed in another part of the building. But it was believed to arouse homicidal instincts in the minds of more than one sensitive Grill customer.

As a result of the murder notoriety the Park Central dropped its advertising overhead from $25,000 to $5,000 per week. But the management thereafter paid more attention to the character of its clientele and frowned upon Broadway wits who wanted the Grill renamed Club Rothstein or the Shooting Gallery.

In December the band was hired for the Lew Fields show *Hello Daddy* and opened in the pit of the Mansfield Theatre. This was a doubling job for it continued to entertain at the Park Central. The band's size was augmented to nineteen men, a bigger crowd than Pollack was accustomed to direct. The duty was assigned to Max Steiner who performed it with extravagant use of the baton and a heavy Teutonic accent which the disrespectful Pollack musicians were quick to mimic. Steiner found them especially difficult to control during the high kick routines. To the drive of Bauduc's drumming the band would begin to boil. Its rapid beat was, of course, rough on the chorus girls. They grew breathless, started to pant and aimed a few unglamorous scowls at the hapless maestro, Steiner.

Hello Daddy required the band to wear full-dress outfits. The suits Benny Goodman and Gil Rodin rented turned out to be waiters' uniforms. Jack showed up in a mismatched jacket and trousers—and wearing a cap. But with their new salaries of about $500 a week they atoned for their earlier shabbiness in excessively debonair fashion, buying the flashiest dress suits, top hats and canes.

The band's new schedule placed it in the Park Central at 6.30 p.m. doing a broadcast until eight, then at the Mansfield Theatre until eleven and back at the hotel for a final two or three hours. The timetable was interrupted briefly at 8 p.m. for a descent into Jeff's Cellar. Jeff's speciality was a threatening blend of gin and grape juice in equal proportions. It was poured into malted milk glasses and imbibed via straws. The musicians smuggled their glasses into the theatre pit by concealing them within their heavy Chesterfield coats. During the seven-month run of *Hello Daddy* the sight of a prosperously clothed bandsman carrying a smart cane and sucking busily on a straw sprouting from his opulent coat became a not uncommon one around the stage-door entrance.

One of the popular *Hello Daddy* tunes written by Dorothy Fields and Jimmy McHugh was *Out Where the Blues Begin.* The band recorded it under the pseudonym of Mills' Musical Clowns and Mildred Roselle, a studio singer, had the pleasure of singing:

> Let me rave and let me riot
> Eating cactus for a diet,
> I can whoopee on the quiet
> Out where the blues begin.

Aside from the regular studio commitments imposed by Pollack's contract with Victor, a segment of the band recorded profusely for smaller, transitory labels like Banner, Oriole, Romeo, Cameo, Lincoln and Perfect. Personnel identities were masked under more than forty different pseudonyms usually dreamed up in the studio. Among the more colourful were the Toe Ticklers, Good Timers, Campus Boys, Ten Blackberries, Ten Freshmen, Ben's Bad Boys, Detroiters, Kentucky Grasshoppers and Sunny Clapp and his Band O' Sunshine.

Attempts were even made to change styles for the various studios. And notwithstanding a frequent sloppiness in arrangements, much robust jazz emerged. Some recording directors were unimpressed. A Banner executive who called on Gil Rodin to negotiate a date was crushingly cool to the good hot performances Gil played for him on the phonograph. At last an exasperated Rodin spun a hoked-up *St. Louis Blues* which the boys had cut in an insane mood and called *Shirttail Stomp*. 'That's it,' yelled the Banner man. 'Just what we want.'

The final agreement permitted the musicians to treat certain tunes as they wished provided they made an equal number of *Shirttail* type cornballs. These usually consisted of barnyard sounds and odd 'icky' musings by the irrepressible Dick Morgan.

In a less whacky, more jazz-flavoured fashion, Jack contributed a scat vocal to *Tight Like That*. By now his unique singing style was being featured on occasional band records. As a rule the studio hired the singers. Sometimes their names appeared on the labels but usually their reward was the same anonymity accorded the musicians. In most cases it was well deserved. Marked individuality was rare and only a handful of singers, like Gene Austin, Scrappy Lambert and Smith Ballew enjoyed any lasting popularity.

Jack's vocal debut on phonograph records was hardly shattering. It followed Jimmy McPartland's opening 'reveille' to *Bugle Call Rag* and consisted of the single hoarse utterance, 'Oh, time to get up and get going.'

Several studio dates later the hired singer failed to show and Teagarden substituted. And here at last, among white male singers, was individuality. His voice gave a wistful laziness to the sentimental ballads, a strong husky *vibrato* to the blues. The phrasing and tone of it seemed a natural extension of his trombone style.

On the non-contractual jobs, Teagarden and his colleagues sometimes called themselves the Pollack Band without Pollack. Many years later, painstaking record collectors, upset by the bewildering shuffle of personnel, generally alluded to them by their most popular pseudonym—the Whoopee Makers.

March 5th, 1929, was cold in New York. Reasonably enough the six musicians who gathered at the Okeh studio around nine o'clock that morning were making constant assault upon the warming jug someone had produced. Jack had been out all night and it was beginning to show. Ed Lang was quietly tuning his guitar. Kaiser Marshall, the drummer, and Happy Cauldwell, who played tenor saxophone, had come down from their Harlem homes. Then Joe Sullivan came in with a third Negro; one whose talents as a hot trumpeter and singer were already appreciated far beyond America's borders. Certainly these men were not conscious that this was to be the initial step towards eradication of the colour barrier from small group studio recordings.

It wasn't Jack's first meeting with Louis Armstrong. Years before in New Orleans, seeking a clarinet player for Peck Kelley, he had heard powerful trumpet phrases soaring from a riverboat at the Canal Street wharf. When Armstrong stepped ashore Jack shook hands with him. This meeting was brief but Jack became thoroughly familiar with Armstrong's memorable mid-'twenties work on records.

Now it was Armstrong's turn to be impressed. While the Okeh engineer limbered up and the unsegregated group booted a few practice choruses he got his first taste of Teagarden's trombone. 'It moves me,' he said later, placing a hand over his heart. 'It moves me right through *here*.'

Louis was undoubtedly moved that morning. He walked slowly around the studio, seeking a spot from which best to hear the trombone sound. He found one at the top of a stepladder near the skylight. The engineer persuaded him to descend for the recording and after a final bout with the jug they bit into a blues as raw as the morning. Then it was over and with a nod at the empty bottle, they called it *Knockin' a Jug*. Over a quarter of a century later it was still regarded by connoisseurs as the purest jazz on record.

It is, too, the most remarkable recorded example of the Teagarden capacity for blues expression, one which, in depth of feeling and effectiveness of phrasing, was at least equal to that of the best Negro musicians. As has been stated, the *feeling* was already there, traceable to Jack's early youth and almost surely a result of his childhood melancholy. The phrasing is at least as intriguing for it reveals a debt—not to Jimmy Harrison, certainly, but to Louis Armstrong. Considering the flexibility of the trumpet and the relative intractability of the trombone, few if any exponents of the latter instrument would ever attempt to repeat jazz trumpet choruses, especially those of Louis Armstrong. There can be no doubt that Jack did not seek to borrow the difficult Armstrong phraseology. It is apparent, however, that sympathetic listening to Armstrong (on records and in Harlem) had implanted certain Armstrong inventions in his mind but not, it should be noted, in his 'regular' style. For during his bandstand working hours with Pollack, Jack's trombone, though called upon for frequent bursts of lively improvisation, was an instrument of popular dance music rather than a medium for uninhibited jazz expression. The Okeh recording studio was scarcely a more appropriate setting for the blues than the Florentine Grill. But the time of day and, above all, the presence of Louis Armstrong, stimulated the release of Jack's unforgettable solos. It was the tail-end of an all night Harlem pub-crawl, the morning bleak and hangoverish. What can be heard of Sullivan's piano above Marshall's drum tattoo suggests a rolling but light quality; and the guitar, even in the sensitive hands of Eddie Lang, is ill-suited for emphatic blues statements. Jack's only major companion soloists were the Negroes Happy Cauldwell and Louis. Cauldwell's contribution evokes the impression of a sax-toting tippler and his mood is one of half-humorous abandon rather than blues urgency. Which leaves Louis. There can be little wonder that the trumpeter was so deeply touched by the white trombonist's solos with which the record begins. He must have been startled by the second Teagarden chorus which, with its repetitive notes (the first four bars) ending with an upsweep, followed by the descending phrase of the second four, echo, in the trombone's broad tones, familiar Armstrong patterns.

The influence of Armstrong in the work of other jazz musicians (and even popular non-jazz favourites) has become axiomatic over the years. But at the time of *Knockin' a Jug* he was not a national figure and only within the previous three or four years had his creative powers reached full development. The traces of Armstrong 'influence' in Teagarden's work during this time are less evidence of imitative devotion rather than spontaneous sympathy. It is difficult not to regard *Knockin' a Jug* as the most exciting proof of the comparable stature of two dominant jazz musicians, mutually inspired, mutually sympathetic, here playing together for the first time.

The rough, almost overtly uninhibited tone of Jack's horn on this recording is as unabashed a statement of the blues as will be found anywhere; and no other record which he made re-captures it so consummately. It will be found, however, to a less inflammatory degree, on some of the Whoopee Maker sessions; those which, the mood plainly confirms, were made by intensely jazz-minded white youngsters still under the spell of all night exposure to the joys of Harlem. It was quite obvious who was the most thoroughly enchanted. Listen, for example, to the *Dirty Dog* date already referred to. Jack's two final trombone essays are splendidly simple blues affirmations, containing in the second chorus, a series of single-note breaks again reminiscent of Louis Armstrong.

This rare warmth is slightly diluted, although the impro-visatory accomplishments are higher on certain records with Red Nichols and other purveyors of 'white' jazz. *Indiana*, for instance, was made only a month or so after *Knockin' a Jug* but the company is different, an air of respectability governing the arranged passages extends to the solos. Nevertheless, Jack employs 'hot', grabbing phrases during the second half of his eight-bar contribution.

In *China Boy* the Windy City mood is chiefly uppermost and inspires Goodman to play in his hottest vein; similarly, the rough-edged treatment of Spencer Williams' old stomp, *Shim-me-Sha-Wabble*. *The Sheik of Araby* emerges as an interesting if obvious contrast in sweet and hot styles. The limp singer opening the number is interrupted in mid-strain by Teagarden who shoves him aside with a husky bit of foolishness. The spirit of contrast prevails with a succession of hot solos super-imposed upon Glenn Miller's straight repeats of the melody.

The droll introduction to *The Sheik* was written by Miller
and Jack following an all-night communion of minds. Both
trombonists got together again at Glenn's home to work out an
arrangement for *Basin Street Blues*. Helen Miller kept them
alert with constant injections of hot coffee and the result of their
joint labour was the now universally adopted preamble:

> Won't you come along with me,
> To the Mississippi.
> We'll take a boat to the land of dreams,
> Heaven on earth, they call it New Orleans.

Jack's work, generally, on the Red Nichols recordings is
closer to *Knockin' a Jug* than to any of the large number of
Pollack band records then flowing on to the market. But even
on the Pollack sides there is enough 'jug' content in Jack's tone
plus his technical facility at improvisation to banish their sometimes plodding mediocrity.

In the late spring of 1929, Ora came up from Texas to join
her husband. She brought little Jack and Gilbert with her. The
family reunion was sweet. It was also doomed. Ora had suffered
Jack's long absences enough back home. But now she was
deprived of the consolation of privacy for her loneliness. His
cronies, male and female, called for him personally and by telephone, spoke of him with what seemed shocking familiarity.
Ora shrank from them, aware that she had lost Jack to the roaring instability which was central New York City, 1929.
Defeated, she and the children turned their backs upon it and
him and returned to Texas.

Meanwhile, another woman waited. Clare too was afraid of
losing Jack. Even after Ora's departure, the anxiety remained.
It was not fear of losing him to another girl but the aching
conviction that he was already lost to a rival far more irrestible.
So long as he had the urge and talent to create jazz, so long as he
carelessly and intemperately sought every opportunity to do so,
no woman would wholly possess him. Ora would not be the
only one to find this out the heartbreaking way.

One night after a broadcast Jack dropped into Plunkett's and called Clare. 'Hear the show?'

'No. I . . .'

'Why not?'

She hesitated. It wasn't easy to tell him the truth, that although she loved to hear him play she was beginning to hate the whole crazy jazz life which kept tugging him away from her.

'Why not?' he repeated, hurt now.

Clare sighed. 'Jack, if you were only a ditch-digger . . .'

'A *what?*'

'. . . or a streetcar-driver. At least I'd be sure of you and . . .'

Jack swore and hung up. Then he turned to Ray Bauduc who was uncorking a bottle. 'Women,' he snorted, and cursed again. Ray nodded in solemn agreement and proffered the bottle.

That week Clare moved to a block on West 47th ironically tagged Dream Alley. Two doors down lived Bauduc and his brother Jules whose high-ceilinged apartment became each night a popular catchall for wandering and dishevelled musicians. And not only musicians. Sometimes show people working round the corner at the Palace dropped in.

The Bauduc flat was also utilized as a kind of hospitable listening booth for those with records to play and discuss excitedly. Clare, a frequent visitor, served refreshments while they circled around a squeaking victrola urging each other to hear this or that hot chorus. Almost without exception, such instrumental solos occupied only a fraction of each record. As it was, of course, unmarked from the rest of the disc's surface, a certain skill was required to lower the needle in the correct groove.

The skill became brilliantly perfected. Repeatedly, for each new guest was ordered to listen, the needle would touch down in the proper groove. The dull orchestration which preceded the solo was left unheard. Although prolonged consumption of gin might limit the capacities of Bauduc's guests in other directions, it never impaired their ability to eliminate the unwanted sludge, without damage to the record, and isolate the jazz chorus they wished to hear.

That summer the band broadcast several shows for Fleisch-
man's Yeast and travelled the New York vaudeville circuit. One
hot afternoon the boys were idling before going on at the Fox
Theatre in Brooklyn. Benny Goodman and Jimmy McPartland
went up on the roof to play handball. They got dustier, sweatier
as the game progressed. Suddenly it was curtain time. Dashing
downstairs they grabbed their instruments and hurried on stage.

Half-way through the show McPartland took a couple of solo
spots out front. Pollack eyed the trumpeter's dirty tennis shoes
and all but dropped his baton. A grim expression settled on his
face. When the curtain fell he stalked over to McPartland and
exploded with threats of dismissal. Then Goodman stepped
forward. If anything his shoes were worse than McPartland's.
Pollack blinked.

'You give Jimmy two weeks' notice,' said Benny gravely,
'and you can give me mine.'

'All right,' roared Pollack. 'He's got his.'

Benny shook his head. His tone was quite mild. 'Well,' he
said, 'I'll take mine, too.'

Jack's dismay over losing his two friends turned into a resentment which some of the bandsmen were already feeling. They
considered many of Pollack's ideas of discipline and commercial presentation nothing but high-handedness and sheer
corn. Nevertheless, a sense of loyalty kept the organization
intact. It had lost two of its most talented members but they
were replaced by another gifted pair.

Acting on reports from Oklahoma that Charles Teagarden
was developing into a first-rate musician, Jack sent for him.
But although the band in which he occupied trumpet chair was
not a commercially enterprising unit, Charles was unwilling at
first to quit it. Then his colleagues persuaded him that this was
his big chance. He headed for New York.

He was met at the station by Clare who was at once impressed
by his good manners and the youthful pride with which he
carried his trumpet case. Jack took him to Pollack who was even
more affected by his playing. A few days later Pollack adopted
another recommendation of Jack's and hired Matty Matlock,

a slim boyish clarinet player from Nashville, Tennessee. The talents of the newcomers were not especially challenged by their first major assignment, a record date at Victor studios to make *Keep Your Undershirt On.*

That summer Jack bought a 1926 Packard tourer. While driving through Brooklyn one afternoon on their way to Coney Island, Clare was seized by the impulse to visit her parents. She had not seen them for several months because of an apprehension that they would disapprove not only of the life she was leading but probably of whom she was leading it with.

She made Jack park around the corner from the Manzi home and went in alone. Her mother greeted her warmly. So warmly, in fact, she decided to tell all. 'I want you to meet him,' she finished. 'You'll like him. You can't help liking him.'

On her way out she felt it necessary to add, 'Just don't ask him any questions.'

Fortunately, Jack was in his most amiable mood. His easy, disarming smile robbed Mrs. Manzi of the instinct to make searching inquiries and within minutes they were all off to Coney Island where he banished whatever doubts lingered by buying more ice cream than any of them could comfortably consume.

They returned to Brooklyn and were joined by Mr. Manzi who drew on his private stock of fine Italian wines to celebrate the reunion. Plans were discussed for a Sunday picnic. 'Let's start early,' said Mrs. Manzi. 'Say about nine.' Jack agreed at once. In this mellow frame of mind he would have agreed to anything.

But Clare was worried. She knew that if Jack was up any time before noon it was because he hadn't been to bed the night before. At such times he was only partially conscious by the afternoon. The favourable impression he had made on her parents, she felt anxiously, was doomed.

She reckoned without an unexpected attack of determination. On the Saturday night Jack got home early and reasonably sober. Next morning he was up at eight. The effort swayed him but slightly and only for a moment. He got into the Packard

and drove off with the air of a man who has faced and conquered
a stern crisis. An hour later Charles was driving and Jack was
in the back seat with Clare's father and a gallon of wine intended
for the picnic. It never got there.

When, shortly afterwards, the Pollack band suffered a layoff,
some of its members including Jack were hired by Red Nichols
for a two-week job at the New Yorker Hotel. Jack was now
living at the Belvedere where the register carried the names of
Bing Crosby, Bix Biederbecke and others from the Paul Whiteman stable. Bing was, of course, one of Whiteman's singers and
had just cut his first solo record *Can't We Be Friends*. When it
was released *Variety* commented: 'Crosby has a peach tenor
that may go baritone with age. Looks like a possible favourite,
properly piloted.' While there is nothing peach-like about
Jack's voice, which had already appeared on numerous recordings, its lazy rhythmic quality is reflected in more than a few
early Crosby hits.

Bix Biederbecke's fame, among trumpeters at least, was already
widespread. The tales of his life and habits are constantly retold
and new ones added. At first Jack found nothing unusual about
him beyond his musical talents. On the afternoon of Nichols'
opening night at the New Yorker, Jack was in Bix's room helping him to get *In a Mist* down on paper. Bix sat before a small
white spinet and it wasn't just *In a Mist*. His fingers raced,
faltered, lingered over the keys and other phrases escaped, some
fevered, some placid. At times Jack whistled a few contributions.
And Bix would nod, yell, and play on. On and on. It grew dark
and still Bix continued playing. Jack felt the spell tighten. He
told himself, it's the gin, and knew it wasn't. It was something
he couldn't define. Perplexity always annoyed him so he didn't
even try defining it.

He shrugged the feeling away and left hurriedly for the New
Yorker. He got there late but in time for a cold rebuke from
Red Nichols.

Later he became aware of Bix's little oddities. His memory
lapses, for instance. Repeatedly he lost his horn. Once after
mailing a letter he walked off leaving the instrument in a paper

bag on top of the mailbox. Jack loaned him a cheap trumpet Pollack had bought for novelty purposes. A year later he surprised Jack by producing it. 'Best horn I ever owned,' said Bix.

One evening Jack looked in Bix's room and found him alone, despondent. He had been drinking, which wasn't unusual, but there was something disturbing in his attitude. Suddenly he asked Jack to drive him to the Bellevue Morgue. Several drinks later they drove off in Jack's Packard. After bribing the watchman to let them in they inspected just one occupant and left in haste.

Years later, long after the strange and gifted Bix had gone, Teagarden barely recalled the aberrations. Instead he remembered *In a Mist* and the small white spinet, and Bix sitting before it, alive with promise and poetry.

November 1929. Of the hurricane that hit Wall Street the Pollack musicians felt hardly a breath. Three weeks after it they were broadcasting from the Silver Slipper, an establishment lately controlled by the mobster Owney Madden. Its present bosses were at least questionable and when one of them got himself shot, the radio network handling the show suffered some embarrassment. In due course the air wire was pulled out of the Slipper and shortly thereafter Pollack quit too.

The impact of the financial crash deepened. Band bookers began shouting their own brand of blues. The jitters spread into every corner of show business including the phonograph record industry. As if to worsen the gloom a new drive was launched against the speakeasies. On New Year's Eve there were nineteen raids in Manhattan alone.

Ben Pollack's band, which had yet to feel the pinch, made a Vitaphone short at Warners' Brooklyn studios. Sound techniques were still in their infancy and errors of synchronization were not uncommon. Not all were as fascinating, though, as in the Pollack film which blared brass while the violins were on screen and produced fiddle sounds from Jack's trombone. Loudly praised by the Pollack boys as the season's funniest comedy, it was withdrawn shortly after its release.

That Christmas, Clare bought a tiny shaggy pup called

Prissy. She also invited the entire Pollack orchestra to a party. It began quietly enough but the steady intake of bootleg liquor transformed it into a sizeable riot. The uproar was compounded by the victrola voices of Louis Armstrong and Bessie Smith while Prissy barked several choruses of her own.

The following spring found the band working for three weeks at the Castilian Royal after which it moved into a Long Island roadhouse called the Duck. Then came another layoff during which most of the musicians went home or sought fill-in jobs. Jack visited his mother in Oklahoma City and took Clare along.

After greeting her son warmly Helen Teagarden introduced seven brawny oil workers as her boarders. In a matter of hours the local musicians heard of Jack's arrival and came around bearing gifts—all bottled. A spirit of celebration descended upon Mrs. Teagarden's household and when Jack and the musicians left for a survey of the city's night haunts, the oil-men fell to quarrelling. Fearfully Clare watched them. They became violent and began overturning the furniture. A stern knocking on the door interrupted them. It was the police summoned by aroused neighbours.

Desperately Mrs. Teagarden begged her boarders to subside. She reminded them of the favours they had enjoyed while lodging on her premises, the savory meals she provided. This took effect. The oil-men paused, their expressions suddenly contrite. But the police could be delayed no longer. Helen opened the door and gave them the familiar genial Teagarden smile. The officers looked beyond her to see seven disordered giants and a woman, all innocent of mien and surrounded by scattered pieces of furniture. The law departed, understandably puzzled, and the oil-men righted the chairs. Tranquillity was restored only to be shattered by the return of Jack with a noisy contingent of the local musicians' union.

Driving back to New York, Jack's long suppressed mechanical inclinations were aroused by a simple blowout. It was mid-afternoon. He fixed the tyre, started the motor and frowned.

'Doesn't sound right, does it?' he asked.

'Yes,' said Clare.

He ignored her and hoisted the hood. Then he lowered it and drove to the nearest hotel. In the parking lot he got to work in earnest. Dusk fell and he rigged up a lamp. Clare went to her room and turned in. Next morning she found him still in the lot, assembling the motor.

'Took it right down,' he said. 'Ought to run easier now.'

'Oh, sure,' said Clare.

But the Packard's days were numbered. The following August it rolled out of the city and north to Saratoga Springs. The Teagarden brothers sat up front, Charles at the wheel. In the rear, band instruments and props were piled high and crowned with Harry Goodman's massive tiger head. Suddenly an elderly lady backed out of the driveway, blocking the road ahead. Instead of righting her vehicle and driving off, she stared at the oncoming car, registered instant fright and stopped dead. Charles swerved to avoid her and tipped the Packard over a shallow cliff where it fell asunder at once. Shaken, the brothers staggered back to the road. The woman had fled.

Jack cursed loudly and pointlessly and flagged three cars none of which stopped. Charles rescued the band's display banner from the wreck and muttered, 'This ought to stop 'em.' He spread it on the road. The next car to come along ran right over it.

'Wait a minute,' said Jack and descended to the remains of his car.

A state trooper making a leisurely reconnaissance along the highway rounded a curve to be confronted with a huge banner bearing the words BEN POLLACK lying in the middle of the road, framed by several jazz instruments and guarded by the head of a tiger.

Accustomed to the unexpected the trooper braked without flinching. Half-an-hour later the two musicians were entering the Albany railroad station with a police escort. As they boarded the train for Saratoga they were given a rousing cheer. But, for a number of passengers, the ride to Saratoga was one of un-easiness as they sat under the fixed and melancholy stare of a monstrous, moth-eaten tiger head.

The band played at Riley's-on-the-Lake for the rest of the summer. Jack, Charles, Matlock, Bauduc and Dick Morgan rented a house which was immediately christened Icky Fraternity. Also in Saratoga for the season were Paul Whiteman and his orchestra. They were playing at the Arrowhead Inn and plainly drawing larger crowds than patronized Riley's.

Riley, in fact, was overheard to make slighting remarks about the relative inferiority of Pollack's band. Fortunately, on the last night of the season, a tipsy millionaire entered Riley's gambling chamber and lost $90,000 on the tables. It was estimated that he parted with a further $10,000 in tips. This substantially narrowed the margin between the Arrowhead's summer profit and Riley's.

While in Saratoga, a spokesman for the Whiteman outfit challenged Pollack's men to a softball game. 'What are the stakes?' asked Dick Morgan. As he spoke in his 'icky' tongue a little time was wasted until Harry Goodman translated. 'A keg of beer,' replied the Whiteman representative.

Some of Whiteman's troop had been professional ball players. Pollack's band was not so well blessed. As for Jack, he contemplated the proposed athletics with dismay. His childhood had offered limited opportunity for outdoor games, and in truth, he had never regretted this for it had sharpened his interest in mechanical engineering. Still, on the appointed Saturday afternoon he was one of the assembled bandsmen, some ill-at-ease in all that fresh air, on a park field near the Arrowhead.

Whiteman was given the honour of being the first to bat. The ball flew at him. He swiped mightily, missed, spun with force and executed a brilliant fall. Unable to resume the game he was helped off the field by a commiserating group which included Bix Biederbecke. Subsequent Whiteman batters acquitted themselves with greater skill. Pollack's team began to worry. To strengthen it Ray Bauduc drafted a bottle washer from Riley's, who was called Rosebud and claimed to be a proficient softball man. It was Rosebud's habit to drain his bottles into one inglorious mixture and sip at it when depressed. Bauduc suggested that now would be a good time to test its strength. Rosebud agreed at once and swallowed half the bottle. When his turn came to bat, Rosebud was sleeping heavily in the shade of a tree. Bauduc was unable to stir him.

A cheer ran out as Jack limped to the plate. The limp was a symptom of apprehension, nothing more. Just before the pitch a car drew up beside the field and out stepped Clare. Without warning Jack she had visited a hairdresser and was no longer a latin brunette. She was a flaming blonde. Jack gazed at her stupefied as the ball rushed at him. He awoke and swung wildly. The bat connected. The ball soared into the air for a clean single. Everyone watched in silent amazement. The double shock was too much. Whitefaced and shaken, Jack dropped the bat and walked off the field.

In the absence of an impartial umpire there was heated dispute over who won the game. Paul Whiteman's claim carried the greater weight. At any rate, the members of each band celebrated the contest that night with much more vigour than they had waged it.

The celebration spilled over into Jimmy Plunkett's when the bands returned to New York. One afternoon Bix told Jack, 'Get your cap. I want you to meet a friend.' They picked up Charlie and drove to Greenwich Village. Bix led them into a tiny chaotic apartment where a slight young man simultaneously smiled and grimaced at a piano. He was knee deep in law books, cigarette butts, gin bottles and sheafs of paper bearing strange scribbles.

Bix minced his way through the litter. 'This is Hoagy,' he said.

Hoagland Carmichael hadn't long left law school in Indiana and was working for an investment banking house. In his spare time he wrote songs. The brokerage business was barely crawling. And the songs he had peddled were proving no fire-raisers. 'Ah, what the hell,' he said by way of greeting to Teagarden. Then he delighted his guests with a one-man concert of crazy lyrics and piano whimsy.

He got up suddenly, groped in a dark corner and found a

mildewing cornet. 'Yours,' he said, tossing it to Charles. Charles
blew a few phrases, Hoagy decorating with piano chords which
skipped and capered around Charles' inventions while Jack
listened with his mouth half opened and Bix leaned back with
his eyes quite closed.

Hoagy tried hard to rescue the popular song from the strangle-
hold of the cliché. In his New York days his tunes were
jazz-flavoured stomps or nostalgic moods. Those that were published appealed only to a dedicated but slightly suspect campus
minority. The great American public still favoured funny hats
and romantic treacle.

Next morning Jack got a call. It was Hoagy. 'We're in business,' he said. 'See you at Victor.'

The recording impresario Irving Mills had arranged a date
to feature Carmichael's latest brainchild. Hoagy plucked a
handful of sympathizers from Paul Whiteman's band and added
other available partisans. In retrospect the line-up is fabulous.
It included Jack, Bix, Jim Dorsey, Pee Wee Russell, Bud
Freeman, Joe Venuti and Eddie Lang. But these names meant
little or nothing to record buyers of the time and of course
were not listed on the label.

They recorded *Georgia on My Mind*. Yielding to Victor
officials who were strongly in favour of hearing the melody
straight, Hoagy sang it that way. The officials were less alert
on *Bessie Couldn't Help It*, recorded the same day. Hoagy sang
the woes of the weak-willed Bessie with explosive solos by Jack
and Jimmy Dorsey.

Early in November Pollack secured a job in Cincinnati. By
cable and phone he recalled the band much like a scoutmaster
rallying his troop and moved into the Gibson Hotel for a
profitable stint which lasted until Christmas. Bowing to continuing fashion, the band's book leaned heavily on simpering
novelties and dismal love laments, a policy which, of course,
paid off. Jack and his friends were consoled by the undeniable
profits, occasional opportunity for solo improvisations, and un-
licensed fun after work.

Record dates gave more liberal scope for jazz activity but

Ben Pollack's Band, Park Central Hotel, New York City, 1928-9. In the back row, from left to right, are Eddie Bergman, violin, Larry Binyon, saxophone, Jack Teagarden, trombone, and Al Beller, violin, while in the front row are Al Harris, trumpet, Harry Goodman, bass, James McPartland, trumpet, Ben Goodman, saxophone, Dick Morgan, banjo-guitar, Vic Briedis, piano, and Gil Rodin, saxophone. Ben Pollack is seated

The last Pollack band in 1933, before it became Bob Crosby's

Paul Whiteman's Orchestra in 1934

here, too, a stringency was imposed by officials who subscribed to the popular and therefore profitable notion that the melody, while framed within ornate arrangement, should be plainly recognizable.

Like the year before it, 1931 for Ben Pollack's band was a crazy twelve months of record dates, hotel jobs, and intervening periods of idleness during which the musicians spent their earnings like water or obtained fill-in work elsewhere. Charles was fortunate in joining Red Nichols' pit orchestra for the Gershwin show *Girl Crazy*. But at the end of each layoff there were always some who were penniless. In order to reassemble his men for a new job Pollack often had to cable the train fare to them.

His pride in the band was boundless and in a sense paternal. He had, after all, fathered the organization and although he was forever alert to its commercial potentials there is no reason to doubt that part of his affection for it had nothing to do with financial profit.

Still, it seemed to Jack then that Ben was becoming less bandleader than businessman. Never truly 'one of the boys' he was acting more like the 'boss'. Together with manager Bernie Foyer, who was like himself, brisk and cocksure, Pollack continued to invent 'popular' novelties in which his musicians participated with mounting apathy.

Except, that is, Dick Morgan, who usually managed to turn the most insipid stunt into an uproarious jape. One of his specialities was a snake dance which he performed with a wired and disturbingly lifelike python. The band moved into a decaying Cleveland dance hall misnamed the Garden. It drew a large crowd despite the caravan of rats which sometimes crossed the floor. 'Must be a hardy mob,' said Dick Morgan. He coiled the snake about his waist and under his coat then wandered casually among the dancers.

At carefully selected moments he opened his jacket and let the snake spring out. The response was at first disappointing. Some dancers tittered but none fainted. Morgan tried it out on the Garden staff with more success. A few hired hands quit at once. Among them was the doorman, a seven-foot giant wearing a blue and gold uniform. He was also an amateur dancer in the Bert Williams tradition and known as Happy. When Happy saw Dick Morgan's snake he upset two tables and fled. The band's stay was shortened at the request of the manager who not only felt the loss of his dancing doorman but was himself somewhat unnerved by 'Icky' Morgan's python.

When Morgan left Pollack he took with him much of the humour which had buoyed the band. He leased his guitar and his comedy to other orchestras before entering the West Coast film and radio industry where he spent the rest of his life. Of his weird 'icky' doubletalk perhaps a few traces passed into general musicians' use. Recitations by the inventor himself appear on isolated collectors' items like *Four or Five Times* and *Icky Blues*. A recorded tribute written by Glenn Miller and called *When Icky Morgan Plays the Organ, Look Out* also exists. This too is an archive piece and best left undisturbed. However, in later years, despite the sophistication which success—or failure—brought to the dispersed Pollack alumni, Morgan's 'icky' cult survived as a fond if lunatic memory.

Morgan was succeeded by Hilton 'Nappy' Lamare, a New Orleans boy whom Jack recalled having heard picking a guitar in an Atlantic City tavern while singing *You're My Big Butter and Egg Man* with an oddly tremulous whine.

When the saxophonist Larry Binyon left, Lamare and Ray Bauduc talked Pollack into a meeting at Roseland with Eddie Miller who was playing tenor sax there. 'He's from New Orleans, too,' Lamare vouchsafed as extra persuasion.

After an audition, Pollack hired him. 'I'll get you a gold horn,' he said.

'Brass is good enough for me,' Miller replied.

'But not for Pollack.'

'Gold horns cost money.'

'Sure.' Pollack nodded. 'You can pay me back out of your salary. In instalments.'

There were now three New Orleans musicians in the band—Miller, Lamare and Bauduc. The shift in personnel balance from Chicago to the Crescent City brought no important change to its style which continued, in public appearances at least, to be utterly 'commercial' though sometimes with a thumping jazz beat. But the alliance of these New Orleans men contributed to the approaching metamorphosis of Ben Pollack's Ballroom Orchestra into Bob Crosby's Dixieland Band.

There were other changes. Gil Bowers succeeded Vic Breidis at the piano. And on the eve of a job at the Summit Inn, Baltimore, Charles Teagarden quit. He was replaced by one Tommy Thunen whose trumpet endeavours, though unquestionably sincere, were unappreciated by his colleagues.

Anxiously Pollack sought a radio sponsor. For the opening show in Baltimore he invited several gentlemen influential in the broadcasting trade and warned his men to be on their best behaviour. Alas, it proved to be an unsettling first night. Ray Bauduc's disgust with Tommy Thunen had been mounting. During the first set, the trumpeter's efforts exasperated Bauduc into yelling, 'What the hell you need is a herring!'

Pollack shot an alarmed glance at his guests and forced a smile to cover up the incident.

Next set, Tommy Thunen walked on carrying a large wet herring.

There was more trouble from the trombone chair. Upon arrival in Baltimore, Jack had, as usual, investigated the boozier sections of town. Now he was on stand, erect enough but in imminent danger of buckling. Pollack lifted his baton for attention. The expectant pause was suddenly shattered as the slide fell out of Jack's trombone. Reaching for it he crumpled noisily against Bauduc's bass drum. Pollack gave a hasty downbeat and the commotion was partly veiled as the band sprang upon *There's A Wah Wah Gal in Caliente*.

Before the next number, Ray repaired Jack's trombone with the aid of a rubber band. Followed by Pollack's hissed order to 'get straightened out', they left the stand, Bauduc leading Jack to the kitchen where he filled a soup bowl with hot coffee. Jack gulped a mouthful. The stuff scalded his tongue and he yelped, flung the bowl forward, drenched Ray's tuxedo, and returned to the stand, jolted into sobriety. Pollack nodded at him, relieved. Then he saw Bauduc's tuxedo. When he turned to his distinguished audience again, Pollack's face still wore a smile. But it was tinged with a definite hopelessness.

Thunen left the band when it opened at the Hollywood Rest in Cleveland. He was replaced by Charlie Spivak, a rotund and skilful horn player who was paired with Sterling Bose. Bose, a wildly intemperate trumpeter, arrived on the job waving a bottle of gin which he invited the band to share.

'I got it off a guy on the train,' said Bose. He swayed and shook his head. 'That poor guy. Gave me the bottle as a gift. What he didn't know was'—he lowered his voice secretively— '*I don't drink.*'

That summer the band went on the road with a Billy Rose show, *Crazy Quilt*, featuring Fanny Brice, Phil Baker and Ted Healy who were described by the *New York Times* as 'stooges assembled in lunatic convention'. In this spirit of madness, the band eagerly joined. Certainly, Sterling Bose needed no coaching in drollery from the *Quilt* cast.

When the band moved into Blossom Heath, a high-class roadhouse near Detroit, 'Bosie' bought an outboard motor-boat. One night he persuaded Teagarden to accompany him on an after-hours fishing trip. They loaded up with gin and chugged out to the middle of Lake St. Claire. While Jack fished, Bose got an urge to clean the petrol line. He dropped it into the lake.

'The hell with it,' said Bose. 'And who needs a motor?' He grabbed an oar and rowed fiercely back to the pier. Jack reached for it. Bose paused suddenly. 'You know,' he said, 'maybe we ought to look for that line.' And he pushed off again. Jack, who was stretching for the pier, missed. He fell into the lake with a quiet splash. Bose rested his oar and shook his head. 'That's a hell of a way to look for it,' he murmured.

The following Sunday morning a posse of federal agents stormed Blossom Heath and seized $10,000 worth of gambling equipment. Over a hundred guests were surprised in the gambling room. Undisturbed, five hundred more were in the swank ballroom being entertained by Libby Holman and Ben Pollack's band. Blossom Heath survived the raid and the band's stay lasted two months.

In the middle of it, word came from Texas that Ora had finally consented to a divorce. Jack and Clare looked up a Justice of the Peace in Wichita, Kansas and were married. Clare had already received discouraging glimpses of life with a jazz musician. It had its unique appeal but the times of despair were many. From that September wedding day she would be even more exposed to the occupational hazards of a band wife.

Travel was one of these, especially in the early 'thirties. When their husbands headed south for an engagement at the Forrest Club in New Orleans, some of the wives, who didn't always join their menfolk on the longer jaunts, decided to follow. Since the Teagarden Packard no longer existed, Clare rode as passenger with Eddie Miller's wife Edna, and Alice Lamare. Each girl had a Ford. For the first leg of the trip Clare rode with Alice. On the back seat sat Clare's hound Prissy and Alice's bull pup named Icky after the guitarist. South of Washington, D.C., they met up with Edna and her three-year-old son Eddie Jr. Clare changed cars. She had some trouble separating Prissy from Icky for a strong attachment had grown between the two. But finally all set off again.

Long before they reached the Gulf of Mexico the two parties had become separated. Somewhere near Tallahassee, Edna turned the car over a ten-foot embankment. The occupants escaped injury with the exception of Prissy, who suffered a slight flesh wound and howled unnecessarily loudly. After unloading their baggage the girls began waving at passing cars. The first to stop was a Ford. It looked familiar. Alice Lamare's head emerged. 'You girls in trouble?' she asked.

'We turned over,' explained Edna.

'You did?' Alice got out and pointed to multiple dents on the roof of her car. 'So did I last night. Four times.'

They all piled in with Alice, and Clare drove the rest of the way to New Orleans where they alighted at the Jung Hotel. After freshening up, they attempted to relate these adventures to their husbands. But their voices were lost in the midst of a hectic New Orleans reunion which Bauduc, Lamare and Eddie Miller were conducting with the Prima brothers and other Crescent City notables.

Back in New York that fall, Jack teamed with Fats Waller in the Columbia studios to make *That's What I Like About You* and *You Rascal You.* The pair exchanged gleeful and sometimes indelicate patter, Fats in the role of the rascal and Jack as the injured husband. Bud Freeman, Tom Dorsey, and the young but gifted guitarist Dick McDonough, added to the fun. The same day, the group recorded two more items, *I Got the Ritz from You* and *Chances Are*, the first of which was never issued. Neither was a record made with Red Nichols some months earlier. But the reason for that reject may be freely conjectured from the title, *Chong, He Came from Hong Kong.*

Six gin bottles became a standard trademark in the studio when Fats Waller recorded; two were placed at the bass and treble positions of the piano, the others strategically located where the flashing hands could capture them between choruses. Gay and irrepressible are the adjectives most often applied to the memory of Fats by his friends—surely he had no enemies. In a profession whose members are not renowned for their sense of marital responsibility, he perhaps was less responsible than most. As a consequence, legal problems fell on him repeatedly. They not only failed to dampen his spirit but left no rancour in his heart. He loved people and liked them to love him. They did.

One morning Clare was feeling uncommonly self-satisfied for having finally got Jack to bed following an all-night excursion. They were living at the Landseer on 51st Street. A sudden knock on the door threatened to shatter Jack's deep slumber. It was followed almost immediately by a contrite tap. Clare opened the door to meet Fats for the first time. He looked embarrassed. 'Beg pardon, ma'am. Could I please talk to Jack?'

'He's asleep,' she replied. 'Is it important?'

'It's awful important, ma'am. Tell him it's Fats.' He stood there huge, shy, and silently pleading.

Clare was helpless. 'Wait,' she said. 'I'll try to wake him.' She returned. 'Not a chance. He's out cold.'

'Well, ma'am,' he stammered. 'You see, what I wanted was—well—I just wanted cab fare up to Harlem. I'm flat broke.'

It happened a hundred times to Fats. All over the country they were playing his songs and scoring them for successful musicals. Royalties piled up into a sizeable fortune. But Fats lacked the cab fare home.

During a spell of work at the Boulevard de Paris, St. Paul, Bose said to Jack, 'We ought to take flying lessons.' It had been an uneventful night. Now it was three in the morning, Jack's hour of negligible resistance.

'Flying lessons? Just what we need.'

Over in Minneapolis one Red Fowler was training commercial airline pilots. He took Jack up in a Stinson and offered to teach him for twenty dollars a lesson. 'Good deal,' said Bose when he heard. 'How do we get to the field every week?'

The answer came from Jerry Johnson, a Texas bass player who had joined Pollack as a replacement for Harry Goodman. 'I'll drive you over,' said Johnson, 'if you'll let me ride along while you're learning.'

The arrangement was satisfactory for ten lessons. Johnson got a free trip and tuition on each. When the instructor decided that Jack and Bose were ready to solo, they suddenly lost interest. But not so Johnson. He asked for and received forty-five minutes extra instruction, then successfully soloed. Ten years later Jerry Johnson was back in Texas teaching R.A.F. pupils to fly.

The Pollack unit dispersed for a lengthy layoff and Jack took a job with the Dorsey brothers in the pit band accompanying *Everybody's Welcome*. Ann Pennington's singing of *As Time Goes By* was one of the show's brighter moments. During the duller spells, Tom Dorsey took his trombone apart and blew spitballs at the audience through the slide. The other musicians watched him with disinterest, until a burly member of the audience seated in the front row grew belligerent. He rose, charged into the pit, collared Dorsey and dragged him into the aisle. A short scuffle took place accompanied by cheers from the orchestra and cast. Ushers separated the combatants, order was restored and the show resumed.

The Pollock band regrouped and moved to Elitch's Gardens in Denver. It was an invigorating spot. Not only was Pollack assured of a nightly average of thirty stations on the radio, but the outlying scenery inspired the wives to an after-hours picnic. They dressed in tee shirts and slacks, stocked up on eggs and beer, trapped their husbands as they left work and drove them protesting up Flagstaff Mountain. Breakfast at a high altitude, dawn over the peaks and beer cooling in a hillside stream soon pacified them. Some were deeply moved. Eddie Miller was heard to murmur that he'd never seen so much nature. Ray Bauduc and Clare suggested a hike whereupon Jack promptly complained of exhaustion and feigned sleep. Ray was extraordinarily active. He charged up the slope with a zest reminiscent of Teddy Roosevelt. Clare followed at a reasonable distance.

Ray yelled, 'What's keeping you?' Then he bounded beyond a rise and disappeared. His shouting ceased abruptly. Clare discovered him moments later near a cactus bush ruefully plucking thorns out of his carcass. Thoroughly disgruntled he limped back to the picnic site where he churlishly shook Jack awake.

A cable arrived at Elitch's from the boss of the Boulevard de Paris. He also owned a club on White Bear Lake, Minnesota. The Plantation was desperately in need of a good band. Would Pollack take the job? Pollack wired consent and opened there a few days later. The event marked an important step in the band's disintegration. The floor show at the Plantation featured an attractive singer named Doris Robbins. Pollack, the phlegmatic businessman, stepped out of character and fell in love. He arranged for Doris to sing with the band on broadcasts and began displaying ideas for her development at the expense of the band. His musicians soon protested but without avail.

An invitation to open at the Belle Reve in Kansas City was accepted. Shortly after his arrival there, Pollack sent for Doris and made her a regular member of the organization. This was too much for the bandsmen. For the first time they had a permanent girl singer. Their distaste was unconcealed, the likely fate of the band was written on the wall in capitals, but if Pollack saw it he took no notice.

After eight weeks in Kansas City they moved on to the Chez Paree in Chicago. The Teagardens found an apartment on North Sheridan and bought a LaSalle car. Like its predecessors, the LaSalle was short-lived. One afternoon it vanished. Jack called the police. 'If you find it,' he finished, 'don't bother me. The damned thing uses too much gas.'

The police called anyway, three days later. The car was an abandoned wreck on the road to Cicero. There were perforations in the rear window and a couple of guns on the back seat.

Despite the recreational excesses common among jazz musicians of the era, Jack retained his boyish appearance and, moreover, was wearing a cap less often. This, allied to his growing popularity as a singer and musician, made him a frequent target for numerous female admirers. A few invaded the hospital room during his recovery from a bout of pneumonia. When Clare heard about it she left in disgust to spend a few weeks with Norma in Oklahoma.

In Chicago the Chez Paree offered a continuous show starring Harry Richman and Sophie Tucker. The Pollack musicians supporting them grew more disgruntled, suspecting now that Miss Robbins was interfering in the band's management. The engagement at the Chez Paree was long and rancorous. Bose left before it ended. He called Jack the following day with a story about a rich acquaintance who was forming a band for the Chicago World's Fair. The way Bose told it, the plans were dazzling, the possibilities exciting. When pressed for details he became characteristically incoherent. But Teagarden was now in a mood to adopt any excuse for leaving Pollack and joined Bose the same day. Unfortunately, the trumpeter's wealthy contact vanished—if he ever existed. The World's Fair dream proved to be an unremunerative job in what was supposed to be a Viennese Beer Garden. Two or three days of this were more than enough. Jack got out fast, sought a speakeasy and righted himself with several double shots. Then he counted his change. It didn't take him long.

'Damn' glad Clare isn't here,' he told himself. He wandered back to North Sheridan. Outside the apartment stood his sister's car. He groaned.

Worse yet, Norma and Clare hadn't returned alone. They had stopped in Oklahoma City and picked up Jack's mother and young brother Cubby. 'Nice to see you,' said Jack. 'Hope you brought your own food.'

He was still puzzling over what—or if—they were going to eat, when Charlie and his wife Drusilla came in. 'We just got in from New York,' said Charlie.

'Nice to see you,' repeated Jack. 'Hope you brought your own food.'

A recording assignment at Columbia's Chicago studio helped out somewhat. It was a shirt-sleeve affair on a hot August afternoon which Jack, Bose, Charles, Tom Dorsey, Bud Freeman and Dick McDonough made warmer by their treatment of *Plantation Moods, Shake Your Hips, Somebody Stole Gabriel's Horn*, and *I've Got It*. The records have historical value today only in so far as they provide interesting examples of Columbia's early attempts to introduce hot jazz to the masses by offering a blend of straight orchestral arrangement and solo improvisation. Since, however, jazz was still regarded either as the exclusive property of the Negro, to be played and appreciated only by him, or as an undesirable contagion from which popular dance music was best free, these essays were not encouraged. *Plantation Moods*, etc., were the first records made by Jack since the termination of his tenure with Pollack. The rough and passionate trombone voice of what may be called his *Knockin' a Jug* phase is all but absent; those brief but glorious months of 1928 through 1930 when he practically dwelt in Harlem, travelling downtown for rest, record dates, and profitable but debilitating intervals on the bandstand with Pollack. Now it was 1933. The influence and novelty of Harlem had palled. Jack had become less a resident than a visitor, then even the visits ceased when Pollack took his band to the mid-west. The tonal strength which had excited Fletcher Henderson and Jimmy Harrison, which had emotionally moved Louis Armstrong was now diminished. On the other hand, Jack's built-in source of gentle sadness (which nothing could remove) had given even the most insipid slow-tempo tunes Pollack's customers demanded a blue sentimentality the composer never considered possible. As vehicles for jazz, they might appear totally unrewarding but, as if by wand-like magic, the Teagarden horn touched them lightly and they became the blues.

Jack, of course, was less concerned with whatever good or bad techniques were acquired by his musical self during his five years with Pollack, than the suspension of steady profits.

Income dwindled and the Teagardens grew restless. Helen, Cubby, and Norma returned to Oklahoma and a square meal. The rest boarded a bus for New York.

Jack had no sooner moved back into the Belvedere when an offer came from Mal Hallett. Hallett, who led an unexciting but successful orchestra, needed a replacement for Jack Jenney. Teagarden considered the bankbook, accepted, and went out on a New England tour.

The band included Gene Krupa, Frankie Carle, saxophonist Toots Mondello, trumpeter Lee Castle, and arranger Spud Murphy. But their talents were not fully encouraged. Even Gene Krupa was forced to play in a rather subdued fashion. Any show of jazz was frowned upon, a policy Hallett no doubt found rewarding. The tour lasted throughout the autumn and consisted chiefly of one-night stands.

Jack's long absence from the rigours of road touring had left him out of condition for such activity. And the Boston brand of bootleg gin lacked any tonic qualities. His health failed and he sought a doctor.

'Musician?' The doctor sniffed. 'Physical exhaustion,' he said and sent Jack to the hospital.

He emerged sufficiently strengthened not only to meet the demands of Hallett's schedule but also to participate in an interesting or even historical series of record sessions.

Some days earlier, John Hammond, a young and wealthy jazz lover and occasional record executive had stepped off the boat from England with a contract in his pocket. It committed him to arrange sixty recordings for an English company. Despite his youth, Hammond was an extremely knowledgeable and opinionated pundit. He knew what he wanted and the passage of time has confirmed that what he wanted was righteous and enduring jazz.

As has been stated, in 1933 such music was not commercially sound. When Hammond approached him, even Benny Goodman was sceptical. Goodman was then occupying an obscure position with a studio orchestra. He was unhappy with the job, but it fed him. When Hammond proposed an all-jazz record series, which was what the English contract called for, Benny demurred. Recalling his Ben Pollack days, he insisted that the only way any jazz could be made commercially acceptable was in the form of limited solos slipped in between arranged passages. Under Hammond's persuasion he entered the deal. For days they wrangled over personnel selection. At last a compromise was reached and a date in mid-October agreed upon.

Hammond's aim was to produce a pure, free-wheeling music with no rigid arrangements or rehearsals, preferably employing undisciplined performers. Viewing the entire idea with quiet alarm, Goodman had special orchestrations prepared. Hammond enlisted Joe Sullivan, Charles Teagarden, and Dick McDonough. He wired Boston for Gene Krupa and Jack who obtained a leave of absence from Hallett and arrived at the Columbia studio as uncertain as the others of just what Hammond and Goodman had planned. They were unimpressed by the staid arrangements of *Ain'tcha Glad* and *I Gotta Right to Sing the Blues*.

As the afternoon wore on, much of the prepared score was scrapped. The musicians felt more relaxed and a warmth crept into their playing. Hammond, of course, was delighted. So was Goodman, although he still doubted the commercial wisdom of 'jazzing up' popular tunes. Teagarden's singing of both tunes made manifest whatever melodic qualities they possessed. This was particularly true of *I Gotta Right to Sing the Blues* which forever after became associated with him.

It was too late in the day to complete the full schedule of recordings. Teagarden and Krupa rushed away to catch their train for Boston but were back a week later for *Dr. Heckle and Mr. Jibe* and *Texas Tea Party*. The first was a Dick McDonough composition, the second a twelve-bar blues accredited to Goodman and Teagarden. Jack sung both, high-lighting the latter with a masterful trombone solo delivered with relaxed confidence but lacking the gruff tension which would have made this a *great* jazz performance.

Although these recordings were made for England, Columbia was urged to release them in America also. They appeared on the shelves a month later and, to everyone's surprise, a few thousand copies were sold. A contract followed for further Columbia recordings under Goodman's name.

On the next two, the Goodman-Hammond group accom-panied Ethel Waters singing two charming numbers from Lew Leslie's *Blackbirds of 1934*. The tunes were *A Hundred Years From Today* and *I Just Couldn't Take It Baby*. Miss Waters' voice was tender and sweet. With less tenderness perhaps but with comparable feeling, Jack sang the same tunes over at Brunswick studios a few days later. This was a date arranged by Victor Young, studio company manager, who had been so enamoured of Jack's voice that he featured the trombonist on the label as a singer only—a signal achievement for a jazzman in 1933.

In the same month, November, he was back at the Columbia studios with Hammond's musicians to make *Your Mother's Son-in-Law* and *Riffin' the Scotch*. It was a memorable session for it marked the recording début of Billie Holliday. She had been working in a small dive on 135th Street. When Hammond found her she was just fifteen and on the threshold of her long and restless career. *Riffin' the Scotch* bore no reference to the fact that Prohibition was about to be repealed.

Another singer, whose career had all but ended, recorded her last four sides in the Columbia studios that same month. But Bessie Smith's voice still dominated all other blues artists and her wrath remained a wondrous thing to behold. Teagarden, Goodman, and a handful of Harlem musicians watched in awe as she bullied Buck Washington, the pianist, then sang *Do Your Duty*. Her voice was powerful but bitterness had quenched much of the fire. And four years later she died as the result of a tragic car accident.

One day the telephone rang in Jack's room at the Belvedere. It was Jack Lavin, Paul Whiteman's manager. Lavin said, 'Paul would like to have you. Say the word and I'll draw up a contract.'

Whiteman had just concluded a year's engagement at the Biltmore Hotel. His was a distinguished society orchestra whose members were highly paid—and regularly. His present trombonists, Bill Rank and Jack Fulton were able readers though not outstanding soloists.

Jack pondered a moment. He was in no frame of mind to go back on the road. His bank account was ailing again. Whiteman's offer was tempting. Like Oscar Wilde, Jack could resist anything except temptation.

'I'll get my horn,' he said. 'Tell Rank to warm a seat for me.'

Clare looked up from her paper. 'Let's see the contract first.'

Next morning they visited Lavin's office at the Park Central. 'Here's the contract,' said Lavin. Jack studied it for a moment, then shrugged and passed it to his wife. Music and *Popular Science* were his speed. To study anything else demanded effort. Especially contract clauses.

Clare read it through. 'It's tighter than a new pair of shoes,' she said. 'And it's for five years.'

'Paul wants it that way. Says it takes that long to break a man in.'

'Five years,' Jack murmured. 'That's a future.'

'So's the salary,' said Lavin.

Jack signed.

Chapter VII

PAUL WHITEMAN was the dominant figure in respectable dance music during the nineteen-twenties and much of the 'thirties. A decade later it became fashionable in critical circles to deride his 'symphonic jazz' as nothing more than pretentious corn, and his 1929 claim to the crown of jazz as a publicity agent's effrontery. The Whiteman influence at once refined and thoroughly devitalized American jazz. With this terse conclusion is Whiteman dismissed. Any attempt to question it might meet with scoffing epithets applied to both questioner and bandleader.

Until Whiteman arrived from the west, polite New York society viewed jazz as a sinful pastime. The term was, of course, used to cover all forms of dance music, not to mention certain types of artistic aberration. Whiteman broadened it still further by his symphonic treatment of popular songs. It is interesting to reflect that although New York applauded him for 'symphonic jazz', Whiteman had previously scandalized Los Angeles by jazzing the symphonies. However, Whiteman's Orchestra (the Christian name was often omitted during this phase of his career) was evidently not considered as a jazzband by the Victor Recording Company. For in its 1923 catalogue it is nowhere listed among the twenty-seven titles headed 'Jazz Dance Records'. It is described instead as a 'Dance Orchestra' with the added intelligence that 'everything it does is characterized by marvellous precision of time, by skilful scoring, and by the equally skilful use of sustained harmony in instruments not occupied with the dance rhythm'.

The concerts Whiteman conducted in Aeolian Hall pacified the Carrie Nations of jazz and convinced most New Yorkers that it could be listened to without apprehensions of guilt. In 1924 his first programme ran a weird gamut from a warmed-over *Dixieland One-Step* through Victor Herbert and Gershwin. This was shamelessly billed as a 'jazz' concert. In case the word sowed doubts in the minds of potential ticket buyers, the advertisers aimed at two most vulnerable spots, patriotism and a sense of fair play, by employing the slogans 'Do Justice to Jazz' and 'Hear America First'.

From that time on, Whiteman took the heat off jazz in more than one sense. The public was easily persuaded to call *his* music jazz while, screened by his and kindred glossy fronts, exponents of the pure 'hot' form continued their explorations. Indeed, Whiteman served not only as a massive shield for bona fide jazz musicians but gave many of them a comfortable livelihood. At one time or another Bix Beiderbecke, Joe Venuti, Miff Mole, the Dorsey brothers, Frank Trumbauer, and George Wettling all enjoyed lucrative if musically restricting employment in the Whiteman organization. Few, though, were committed to as long a period as five years in the same stable.

As the economic depression deepened, jobs became scarcer and briefer. Nowhere in America was there any measurable appreciation of creative jazz artists. The public was almost entirely unaware of their existence. Jazz musicians and their respective abilities were known only to one another. Although Jimmy Dorsey could say with justification, 'I think it is artistic suicide for a jazz musician to work with society orchestras,' not to do so was to risk suicide from malnutrition. Hunger drove many musicians to jobs which they despised.

The record business had not fully recovered from the bankruptcy and collapse of the Columbia Phonograph Company but radio was thriving and the studios needed musicians. Benny Goodman joined a group backing the crooner Russ Columbo and

A 1934 photograph of Jack Teagarden when he was with Whiteman

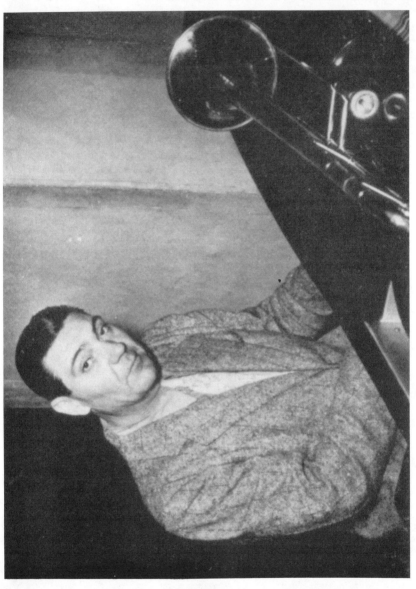

Jack Teagarden in late 1939, just after he had entered the worrisome 'big band' field

at least was able to play music. A few less fortunate contemporaries were consigned to the sound effects department. One noted Chicago drummer was required to produce gun-fight noises from his equipment for a weekly gangster show. To his credit, he walked out of the studio after a few long months.

By signing on for five years, Teagarden insured himself and Clare against privation. On the way home from Lavin's office no fear crossed his mind that his freedom of expression might be cramped by the necessary discipline of a large and complex unit such as Whiteman's. He knew that this was bigger than joining Peck's Bad Boys, bigger than Doc Ross, bigger than Pollack. But still, it was a job. He was twenty-eight, he could read well and 'fake'. Whiteman had sent for *him*. He hadn't sought out Whiteman. It was therefore reasonable to assume that Whiteman considered him the best.

And as he walked into the Belvedere it entered Jack's mind that he *was* the best damned trombone man in the country. It was too much effort to dislodge the notion so he smiled to himself smugly and let it take root. It was bruised only slightly on his first day's work with Whiteman.

The band was working at the Paradise at 49th and Broadway. Rehearsals began at ten in the morning. When Jack got there, thirty musicians were already rehearsing under the direction of Roy Bargy, the pianist. Whiteman hadn't yet arrived. Teagarden lounged against the wall listening approvingly for some moments. Bargy waved the band to silence, turned to Teagarden and said, 'Like it?'

Jack smiled easily and nodded. 'Sounds fine.'

'It should,' Bargy roared. 'We've been rehearsing for thirty minutes minus some damned trombone player who probably can't read a note!'

Jack's grin faded and he meekly took his place in the brass. Thereafter, when Bargy was directing, Jack displayed an uncharacteristic punctuality.

Whiteman was less of a disciplinarian than Bargy and, in a sense, was an image of his own orchestra. He was physically bulky, professionally talented, and possessed uninhibited traits just as the band contained uninhibited musicians. Upon occasion both broke loose. In public he was a natural show-man and sought to impress. And impress he did, at times with less dignity than pomposity. The same can be said of his orchestra.

In the great days, when he took in nearly three quarters of a million dollars a year (paying out a quarter of a million in band expenses), Whiteman was known as a lavish spender and an easy touch. He was not easily deceived but experienced a quite selfish pleasure in being over-generous. Once his manager chided him on the extravagance of his habits. He was spending twelve hundred dollars a week. 'What of it?' replied Whiteman. 'Life is short enough, isn't it? I believe in living while I live.'

He also believed in the infallibility of his own judgement; certainly a reasonable egotism arising from a lifetime of experi-ence not only with musical developments but also with the temperament of his musicians. Roy Bargy once expressed the opinion that with men like Teagarden and Beiderbecke, Paul knew he was dealing with creatures of unusual talent and forgave them more readily when they went a 'little overboard'. Happily, he not only forgave them. Sometimes he went a 'little over-board' with them. He soon found in Jack all the qualities which he demanded of a drinking companion, not the least of which was vertical endurance. In fact, Paul so often sought Jack's society that the latter protested. 'It doesn't look good,' he told Whiteman. 'The boys'll think you're playing favourites.'

'I'm paying you, ain't I?' Whiteman snorted. 'Ain't I paying you?'

Teagarden admitted he was.

'Then come along and don't give me no back talk.'

One day at rehearsal they were running through some Gershwin when Jack's lip faltered. The mistake was distinctly audible. The band lapsed into silence at a grandiose gesture from Whiteman who proceeded to chastise Bill Rank for the fluff. Jack interrupted. 'Wait a minute—that was me, not Bill.'

Whiteman turned to him and scowled. 'Will you keep out of

this and let me do the talking?' he said. 'If I say Rank fluffed, then Rank fluffed. Understand?'

Fortunately, Whiteman's men knew when and when not to take their boss seriously. And if his efforts at imposing personal discipline upon them sometimes fell into simple buffoonery, the benefit they derived from his professional experience and direction cannot be denied. Jack was soon to learn, however, that his progression from the loosely knitted Pollack band to the complex Whiteman organization was by no means an easy one. He found that he was less an individual performer than a cog in a machine. Hitherto accustomed to being the entire trombone section, he was now one mere member of a trombone quartet perched out on the rear wing of an ornate and giant bandstand. It is true that Paul, not unaware of Jack's improvisatory impulses, often permitted him a brief solo which he performed standing up. Unable, however, to extend or develop these solos, he released them with apathy and sat down in frustration. After a while he began to feel like a vaguely discontented jack-in-the-box. Even the gyrations of Sally Rand, who had come to the Paradise fresh from her triumph at the World's Fair, failed to titilate him.

Temporary relief came in joyful fashion from a friendship which he formed with another new-comer to the band named Johnny Mercer. Mercer hadn't long arrived from Savannah and possessed not only a warm southern singing style but a marked flair for composition. Only recently in concert with Hoagy Carmichael, he had won an A.S.C.A.P. award for the tune *Lazybones*.

Mercer's purpose in Paul Whiteman's orchestra was nebulous, for his instrumental prowess was meagre. But he worked out several droll routines in at least two of which, *Fare Thee Well to Harlem* and *Christmas Night in Harlem*, Jack participated with lazy vocals and genial banter. Mercer's popularity was further bolstered by some admirable marksmanship in flicking lighted cigarette butts at Miss Rand's bubbles.

Shortly after Mercer's arrival, Whiteman signed up another Teagarden—Charles. Swiftly and with painstaking sincerity,

Charles absorbed some of the more ticklish arrangements planned for a forthcoming concert. He was vastly more respectful of rehearsals than was his elder brother.

Jack and Johnny did *Fare Thee Well to Harlem* on the stage of the Metropolitan Opera House one December evening and it provided the only straight-forward bit of musical fun on the programme. Whiteman called the show *Experiment in Modern Music*. Jack, via muted horn solo, managed to inject some of his unique feeling for the blues into a highly elaborate Fud Livingston arrangement of *St. Louis Blues*. Charles contributed some appealing passages to *Park Avenue Fantasy*, a Signorelli-Malneck work whose theme survived as the hit tune *Stairway to the Stars*.

1934 began favourably for Jack. Prohibition was repealed and Paul Whiteman went back to the Biltmore for another year. His contract was renewed under terms still more generous than before. He was assured of $4,000 weekly. Other hotels too were offering expansive guarantees to their attractions. They could afford to with the soaring profits from legitimate liquor sales. The year was barely two months old before a large number of citizens were longing for the 'good old days' of bootleg whiskey.

But the Biltmore had tone, no doubt about it. Its supper-room was redecorated for Whiteman's return and renamed the Casino Bleu. Moreover, as the guests sipped their champagne (at nine-fifty a quart), they were treated to a more cerebral brand of music than was customary in Manhattan supper-rooms. The gala opening night was attended by most available celebrities, some of whom, like singer Mildred Bailey, were pressed to perform.

The following Sunday, Whiteman organized the first of a series of Sunday night dinner concerts. Heavily arranged medleys such as *Waltzing Through the Ages* and *Gershwin Favourites* offered no great challenge to either performers or audience. Neither did Morton Gould nor Ferde Grofe. But when Paul led the band into Ravel and Debussy, Jack grasped his horn more tightly and followed the score with infinite care. The instinct to 'add things the composer had never written' plagued him constantly. It was a struggle to suppress it.

One night after work he joined Roy Bargy over a drink. They sat in silence for a while. Then Bargy said, 'It isn't easy for you, is it?'

'I can read the stuff. You know that.'

'Sure I know. But your instincts don't lie in that direction. You'd like to cut loose more often, wouldn't you?'

Cut loose? The expression triggered another of Jack's memories and he chuckled and remembered Peck 'cuttin' a frog'. He spoke the phrase aloud.

'Beg pardon?' said Bargy.

'It's an expression we had down in Texas,' explained Jack. He told Bargy about Peck. He wondered what Peck would have said had he heard him building the monotonous edifice of Ravel's *Bolero* in the Biltmore tonight. He said, 'Be something if we cut a frog on *Bolero*.'

'Might improve it,' mused Bargy.

'Might at that.' He finished his drink quickly and went home to Clare.

These days she was shopping for furniture. The prospect of a year's unbroken tenure in one town, plus the advantage of a regular and substantial pay cheque had encouraged her to set up a home of some permanence. She selected a three-room apartment at the Park Vendome on West 56th. Jack examined it briefly. 'All it needs is a bar.' They moved in. Unfurnished, it was rented for $125 a month, no small amount in 1934.

Jack got his bar and Clare went on a shopping spree which netted some elegant furniture, blue drapes, and an ivory telephone to which Jack took an instant dislike. He had always nurtured a mild hostility towards telephones anyway, although he wasn't sure why. But for the first few days after they moved in, the instrument worked overtime. Calls were made to friends and acquaintances in and out of town. Two hundred dollars' worth of recently repealed liquor and a comparable quantity of food was ordered. Its consumption proved to be one of the most memorable housewarming parties of the Depression days. Jack invited the entire Whiteman school along with such earlier classmates as Jimmy McPartland, Sterling Bose, Bud Freeman, and Benny Goodman. Wives, girl friends, and gatecrashers swelled the function. Many of the guests were working steadily and for comfortable salaries. Others, with no idea where their next meal was coming from when they left, furtively filled their pockets with scraps of food. Some had well-paying radio jobs the next morning. Others could recall with a self-conscious shiver the recent *Variety* headline 'Get the bread-lines off Broadway'. That chill January night at Jack's place it was impossible to tell the down-and-outers from the prosperous. These men all moved in the ever-widening circle of his life. All were there to wish him well and sample his liquor. They did both with gusto. The party lasted for two days and two nights and received honorary mention in the *Metronome*.

When the last guest departed, Jack swept Clare into his arms. Viewing the shambles, he grinned. 'Now it *looks* like home.'

Although the rewards were financially satisfying, the schedule tightened as the sessions at the Biltmore alternated with shows at the Capitol Theatre; broadcasts and rehearsals were somehow squeezed in. Though not a tyrant, Whiteman knew the value of frequent appearances and insisted that no member of his organization needed liquor to inspire a performance. But the demanding grind forced several to test whatever sustaining qualities alcohol possessed. Jack in particular became aware of a gnawing tension, partly the result of the restraints imposed upon his musical urges by Whiteman's inflexible arrangements. And the more his artistic freedom was curtailed, the deeper he slipped into the social liberties of earlier days.

Clare fell sick and during the first few days of her confinement in the hospital Jack was the most attentive of husbands. But as her stay lengthened into weeks, he was afflicted with spells of loneliness and sought remedies which, while fleetingly effective, were not likely to meet with Clare's approval. One of them was a blonde, known along Broadway as Patsy.

An iciness formed between Jack and his wife which each

deplored. They were unable to come to terms and Jack's absences from the apartment increased. That summer, Norma came up to spend a few days with Clare. The vacation was shattered one August morning when Clare's brother called and announced simply, 'Pop's dead.'

Clare crossed town to Brooklyn where the Manzi family gathered together in its grief. Her relatives glanced curiously at Clare and if they wondered where her husband was, they didn't ask. Suddenly the door opened and he came in, almost shyly. He crossed to Clare and reached for her hand. He was sober and suitably crestfallen. During the funeral his behaviour remained above reproach.

The widening gulf between Clare and Jack was being studied with some hope by a musician in Irving Aaronson's band. He was Red Jessup, a trombone player. Red now decided that the time was favourable to confess his feelings which had been for nearly a year tantamount to love. 'If you'll divorce Jack,' he told Clare, 'I'll marry you.'

Red's proposal did not exactly take Clare by surprise but she felt unprepared for weighty decisions just then. And, having suffered the uncertainties of life with one trombonist, she was not over eager to plunge into marriage with another.

But Jessup became persistent. From wherever he happened to be playing he repeated his proposals, often by long distance telephone. From them, from the tangle of her marriage to Jack, from the depression of her bereavement, Clare fled to Chicago and her sister Elaine. Jack went down to the Decca studio and with Sterling Bose, recorded *The Bathtub Ran Over Again*.

It had been a tough summer. Although he could not consider his problems with Clare of pressing importance (and he tried to), they rankled. The three-room apartment at the Park Vendome had lost its attraction and the relentless Whiteman routine was becoming a soul-wrenching grind.

It had not been an unprofitable summer. His weekly salary sometimes exceeded $450. Recordings outside the Whiteman domain had caught on. During one of these dates he stepped beyond orthodox instrumentation and included a young harpist named Caspar Reardon whose playing added an oddly wistful touch to *Junk Man*. Equally appealing was a quartet of sides he made with the Benny Goodman Columbia group. One of the titles, *I Ain't Lazy, I'm Just Dreaming*, perfectly suited his vocal style and came delightfully close to expressing his own attitude toward life.

The records he made with Paul Whiteman that summer were indistinguished popular items such as *Love in Bloom* and the Cole Porter material from *Anything Goes*. In September he recorded *Stars Fell on Alabama*. This was a pleasantly simple melody and one of the season's popular hits. It proved to be one of the best examples of Jack's relaxed singing style. Its charm seemed doubly apparent twenty years later when popular songs were being sung with echo-chamber stridency, or near-contemptuous indolence. The unforced quality of Jack's delivery of *Stars Fell on Alabama* could be described as lazy, but was soothing rather than soporific and, as always, listening to it one felt that the blues was not far away.

In later years, Jack made other recordings of the same tune but none equalled that amiable little Brunswick session in the autumn of 1934. His singing betrayed no trace of his personal problems.

Somewhat to his surprise, Jack was annoyed by Clare's defection. The reasons were twofold. He genuinely missed his wife and he strongly resented losing her to an inferior trombonist. To retrieve her, he was prepared to go to any lengths. He crossed over to Brooklyn in a heavy rainstorm and called on Clare's mother. She listened to his appeals for help but busied herself getting him into dry clothes. Finally, he turned to Clare's brother Leo. 'She'll listen to you,' he said. 'Make her come back here.'

Off Leo went to Chicago. Jack returned to mid-town New York and because he felt a cold coming on, went into a bar. The first two drinks restored him physically but a depression settled upon him. He was in this mood when Ray Bauduc, Charles Spivak, Matty Matlock and others of the now defunct Ben Pollack academy trooped in. After the band's break-up,

Pollack had established himself on the west coast trying to nudge Doris into the films. His musicians made several attempts to regroup, but without success.

'Without a name, we're nothing,' said Bauduc. 'We've driven all the way from California to ask you. . . .'

'Take over, Jack,' urged Matlock. 'With you out in front we can get back in business.'

Teagarden shook his head. 'Haven't you heard? I'm tied to Whiteman for four years.'

'Ask him to release you.'

Jack downed another drink, braced his shoulders and got on the phone. When he returned, his friends read the answer in his face. 'He says I'm valuable property . . . he's got plans for me.'

Like a procession of mourners they left the bar and made for Jack's hotel. All night long they drank and talked over old times and how it could be again if—and they checked the hopes which rose and swept them down with liquor and after a while someone was crying but nobody could tell by then whether it was because of the liquor, the memories, or the drowned hopes.

Later, of course, a name was found to front the band, but that of a man who hardly knew one end of a baton from the other and whose sole benefit as a leader then rested upon the name of his brother. But Bob Crosby realized his musical limitations, sang infrequently, waved a baton with growing confidence, and gave the band full freedom in arrangements and presentation. As a result the Bob Crosby Orchestra was very soon nationally renowned for its excellent musicianship and authentic jazz flavour.

Jack Teagarden, who might have been its leader, continued to serve within the Whiteman corps and struggle with the dilemmas of his and Clare's estrangement. In Chicago she listened as Leo stated her husband's case and finally returned with him to New York. During the journey she had time to review life with Jack and the sum of her reflections was that his wayward traits were neither iniquitous nor deliberate but rather like the errant mischiefs of a small boy. She reached New York in a generous mood although not an entirely forgiving one and she booked in at the Chesterfield Hotel. Jack was staying at the Plymouth. She displayed no impatience to call him. Let him languish a little longer, she felt, which was no more than he deserved. He had, after all, sent for her. But at last she picked up the telephone and got through to his room.

'Hello?' replied Patsy.

It was small wonder that when Irving Aaronson's band returned to New York, its red-headed trombone player found his chances with Clare immeasurably improved. Jack, genuinely irked by Clare's inability to realize that Patsy was nothing more than a passing fancy, took steps to enlighten her. Red Jessup's intrusion blurred the dispute and as a confusing factor, Red had to be eliminated. With this aim in mind, Jack paid a late night visit to the Paradise where Aaronson's band was working. An unusual belligerency in his manner drove the whole orchestra into making a hurried exit and it returned only after he had been ushered from the premises. The incident was widely reported around Manhattan the next day. This marked the only occasion when the local press in describing Jack omitted the adjectives 'genial' or 'amiable'.

Jack altered his approach. He called Clare and asked her to arrange a meeting with Red. 'These things have to be discussed in an adult, man-to-man fashion,' he said seriously. Red Jessup, whose professional admiration of Jack was boundless, agreed to the meeting and the two met in Clare's hotel room. There were handshakes, strained nonchalance, and a few inconsequential exchanges. 'I'll give you ten minutes to talk things over,' Clare said. Then she withdrew. Half an hour later she discovered them sitting in their shirtsleeves facing each other across a bed littered with two trombones and a number of gin bottles. Their speech was thick and rambling, but unmistakably friendly and mostly about music.

Upon seeing Clare, Jack straightened. 'Red,' he said with sudden and unconvincing sternness, 'I got to ask you some questions. Got 'em written down somewhere.' He blinked around the room. 'Doesn't matter. I remember 'em . . . Do you love Clare?'

The question shot out unexpectedly and Jessup jumped. He recovered and answered, 'Of course. Do you?'

It was Jack's turn to be jolted. He took a drink. 'I dunno,' he said. Neither man being in a condition to resolve the impasse which had been so quickly reached, the meeting broke up with smiles and another round of drinks.

'It's no use,' Clare said after Jessup had staggered out. 'It's all over. This time for good.' They discussed how best their property should be apportioned and only on the matter of Prissy's ownership was there any serious disagreement. Both wanted the dog. Reluctantly Jack yielded. By now he knew that his long date with Clare had ended.

He was not given to thoughtful review and as the proper legal steps to terminate their marriage were being taken, life with Clare flashed through his mind, leaving no more impact than the memory of yesterday's recording session. The relationship had begun at an up-tempo but changed to a blues in mid-chorus. Now it collapsed with a dismal coda in the divorce courts.

Clare demanded no alimony. As she well knew, alimony assaults are practically an occupational hazard among jazz musicians and she was proud of her magnaminity. Nor was Jack's pride unaffected. The Whiteman band was playing at Charlotte, North Carolina. Jack sat alone in a local bar when Roy Bargy walked in and joined him.

'She did it,' Jack mumbled. 'She married the guy.'

'Why not?' Bargy asked. 'You're through, aren't you?'

'Why not?' Jack looked up. 'He doesn't even play good trombone.' He never learned that Jessup later joined Rudy Vallee's orchestra. What that knowledge would have done to his already injured pride is beyond speculation.

For some time after Clare's departure, Jack was permitted little opportunity for regrets. The triumphant but demanding Whiteman tour continued. 'Travelling with Whiteman,' the leader's manager said of those days, 'combined the best features of a ball club, a minstrel troupe, and a floating crap game. Stud poker at as high as twenty dollars a card was the standard diversion and the boys put the railway porters to bed and played all night.' But they found time for intensive rehearsals and presented a glittering, highly disciplined pageant on stage. 'Class,' a critic wrote, 'is written all through the Whiteman offering, with the King of Jazz leading the greatest galaxy of individual entertainment he has yet put on display.'

Travel was interrupted each Thursday for the Kraft Music Hall radio show. In the summer of 1934 Whiteman enlivened the production with brief guest spots from various alumni including Mildred Bailey, Joe Venuti, George Gershwin, both Dorseys, and Bing Crosby. In the autumn he tied himself to Kraft for a third year at a salary which jumped from $4,500 to $5,000 weekly.

Although Whiteman was still referred to by the title bestowed upon him five or six years earlier, his was a show band, not a jazz band. He contributed a feeble twelve minutes' music to an unsuccessful Fred Allen film called *Thanks a Million*, while the most significant event in true jazz history since the closing of Storyville was taking place in the Palomar Ballroom, Los Angeles. Benny Goodman signalled his band into a hot Fletcher Henderson arrangement, turned to the dancers and to his surprise found them jumping. A revolution in popular music had started. Swing was here.

It was of course jazz, big band jazz with an emphasized beat and a sophisticated polish. Other bands swiftly joined the trend. But swing, a natural rhythmic ingredient of all jazz since the form's misty origins, remained absent from the Whiteman repertoire.

One morning in November 1935, Manhattan's drama critics were trying to find adequate adjectives to describe a show called *Jumbo* which had just opened at the Hippodrome. '*Jumbo*,' wrote one, 'is a new and startling form of drama. It teems with players who swing by teeth or toes from high trapezes, sing love songs while riding horseback and act a romantic melodrama of circus life to music by Paul Whiteman and a steam calliope.' Less-controlled reviews employed such terms as 'colossal', 'a gaudy tumult', 'delicious wonder', 'an eye-punching pageant', and 'one hell of a show'. Not surprisingly, it was a brainchild of Billy Rose. Ben Hecht and Charles MacArthur provided a weak plot while Rodgers and Hart wrote the songs, only one of which (*My Romance*) has survived. The spectacle was the thing. The interior of the theatre had been completely redecorated in red, white, blue, and gold. Even the seats were scarlet striped and star spangled. The cast included Jimmy Durante, a llama, four lions, numerous horses, a vast assortment of circus acrobats, a huge elephant called 'Big Rosie', and Paul Whiteman. Astride a large white mare Whiteman rode on to the accompaniment of a deafening fanfare from his musicians. One journalist found the bandleader 'an eye-aching vision of glory'.

Thereafter, on subsequent nights, a careful watcher might have observed the maestro gently tickling his steed on the ear with a riding crop. The response was passive for several weeks.

But one evening her patience vanished. With a bored, side-long glance at her rider, she reared, snorted, and amid the guffaws of the audience, proved herself an adept rodeo pony. Still gamely playing, Jack and the other musicians quickly retreated from the flying hooves. Whiteman clawed the air to retain his balance and dignity. Bill Rank, engrossed by his boss's plight, backed into the embrace of Frank Trumbauer's cymbals. His trombone clattered to the floor. The evening and Whiteman's ego were saved by an alert roustabout who hastily lowered the curtain.

After the first few weeks of the show, Jack Teagarden viewed the whole affair as a colossal, eye-punching bore. The public obviously felt the same. The show grossed $18,000 the first night but did steadily less well. The word around Broadway was that 'you just can't mix silk and fertilizer'.

But Jack was making money. Broadcasts from Radio City Music Hall and recording commitments continued to boost his salary. His stoicism was tested by *Look for the Silver Lining*, *A Waltz was Born in Vienna*, and *The Wheel of the Wagon is Broken*. But he played them with both upper and lower lip stiffened.

There were moments of relief from the oppressive schedule. Once, just before going on the air, Paul Whiteman lifted his baton to lead the band into *Chinatown, My Chinatown*. A last-minute impulse seized him and he switched the command to *China Boy*. A rustle of paper sounded coast-to-coast as the musicians changed their music while the red light flashed on. The baton fell and a chaotic burst of discords went out over the air-waves. Without panic, Whiteman realized that the men in the rear hadn't heard him. Softly he directed the band back to *Chinatown*. But by now the *China Boy* order had filtered from the front line to the more remote members. When Whiteman again gave the downbeat, the stunning clash of chords was repeated. Whiteman's self-control ebbed. And just then the restraining screw on his podium came loose, the heavy top crashed to the studio floor. Whiteman roared. But by now he was safely off the air.

On another occasion Whiteman was to accompany a concert *diva* singing three thousand miles away. For its day, this was a bold experiment in radio broadcasting. The engineers, leaving nothing to chance, insisted that each musician wear a set of headphones to enable him to hear the singer. Whiteman objected. His were trained musicians. They would instantly obey his every signal. There was need, therefore, for only one set of headphones. His own. Alas, as he swung his baton downward, it caught the wire lead connecting the headphones to the control booth. The phones were given a sharp twist. Whiteman tried to straighten them while continuing to conduct his band. It was no use. The sight of their leader, one headphone in the middle of his forehead and the other on the back of his head was too much for the band and its performance slid unmusically to a halt. The *diva* sang on magnificently, unaware of the chaos on the east coast and quite unaccompanied.

In the summer of 1936, Billy Rose hired Whiteman for his show at the Texas Centennial Exposition. Naturally, everything had to be big. The fairground amphitheatre seated over five thousand and had a revolving stage large enough to hold a city block. A hundred and twenty-four chorus girls pranced in front of scenery sixty feet high. Whiteman clad himself in a gaudy cowboy rig with a gigantic stetson and a brace of pearl-handled six-shooters. Completing the Western motif, he leased a ranch bigger than the amphitheatre. As if Whiteman's mighty team wasn't sufficient, the Centennial promoters engaged Joe Venuti's Orchestra as an extra attraction.

The two bands faced each other. At the start of every performance the stage lights were extinguished and the entire scene darkened except for Whiteman's baton which was illuminated like a slender will-o'-the-wisp. A flourish of it and his orchestra struck a mighty chord. Venuti's musicians followed with another pitched a half-tone higher. The chord-building continued until one of the bands became exhausted whereupon both would launch a mass assault on *The Eyes of Texas are Upon You.*

Venuti soon tired of his ex-employer's showmanship. One warm evening when all was in readiness, Whiteman's baton swept downward and his orchestra voiced the opening chord. In reply came the forlorn wail of a lone bass saxophone. Then Venuti made his appearance carrying a ten-foot pole from whose end dangled a dazzling five-hundred-watt bulb. If this did not panic the audience, Whiteman's enraged reaction did. He dropped his baton, whipped out his pistols and blazed away at the Texas stars.

After the show, Jack walked home with Venuti. Recent rains had churned much of the ground into soupy mud and planks had been laid for an improvised walk. Both men were in an appropriate centennial mood. During an energetic frolic, Venuti pushed Jack off the plank into the mud. Jack struggled to his feet, laughing, while Venuti strolled on. Two strangers slipped out of the shadows, ranged themselves on either side of the trombonist, and muttered, 'We'll get him for that, Jack.'

'Get him?' Jack blinked. 'We were just kidding around. We . . .'

'Shut up,' one of them snarled. 'Nobody can push a Texan around and get away with it.'

'But he didn't mean . . .'

'I said shut up,' said the man and pointed a gun at him. The pair forced Jack into their car and demanded Venuti's address. Jack said he didn't know it. They drove to the amphitheatre, got Joe's address from a watchman and headed into town. They hammered on Venuti's door and Sally Venuti poked her head out.

'Friends of Joe's? Just a moment while I slip on a robe.'

Deciding the moment was ripe to warn Joe, Jack began singing and staggering like a drunk. He managed a few bars of *Woe is Me*, one of the season's more popular songs, praying meanwhile that Joe would get the message. Joe didn't, but a pair of policemen came on the scene to investigate the disturbance. They recognized Jack's captors as a pair of local hoodlums, relieved them of their hardware and gently ordered them home. Then they turned to Jack. 'Musician, huh?' one said. 'Always breakin' the peace.' And they hustled him off to jail, where he spent the long night reflecting on the wonder of Texas hospitality.

After a stint at the Florida dog tracks, Paul Whiteman took the orchestra back to New York. Seeking relief from big band work, Jack, Charles, and Frank Trumbauer opened at the Hickory House and billed themselves as 'The Three Ts'. None of them needed the extra salary which the after-hours job on 52d Street afforded, but each thirsted for the opportunity to play with a small unit. 52d Street was at the height of its brief, noisy fame as 'Swing Street'. Much of the music which fairly leaped out of the doors of the Onyx, the Famous Door, and Jimmy Ryan's, came from swing-band splinter groups or, less frequently, temporary refugees from outfits like Paul Whiteman's. It was not hard to see the effect which the environment of the latter had upon such essentially 'hot' musicians as the Teagardens. Their playing failed to lift the roof from the Hickory House and the job soon folded. 'The Three Ts' retreated to Whiteman and entertainments like *Cuckoo in the Clock, Mexican Jumping Bean*, and *Slaughter on Tenth Avenue*.

The handful of genuine jazz lovers then existing were pained

Peck Kelly in 1935, with Jimmy Dorsey and Bob McCracken, Dorsey's clarinettist of the time

Jack's big band in 1940, with Norma (piano) just behind the leader

Jack Teagarden with Louis Armstrong

by the noticeable decline in the zest of a man they had long regarded as a giant in music. Otis Ferguson, one of the most articulate of these, noted that, though still a fine musician, '[Teagarden] seems tired and cynical, his creation a bit shopworn. Word about him is always going round. He was with Whiteman in the long stretch of *Jumbo* and it was getting him down and he was taking more heavily to drink. . . . Then they were on the road for months and I saw him in Miami where they were playing a slew of marches for the greyhound races and it struck me that Jack did not like marches or greyhounds either, and it didn't help any when he put a dollar on a dog out of sheer boredom and the pooch would stop and go to work on a flea somewhere around the backstretch.' After summing up Jack's achievements prior to his entry into the Whiteman stable, Otis Ferguson reassured himself with the remark, 'It would be a far far better thing to be Jack Teagarden today, I think, blowing it out listlessly with Whiteman and perhaps hung over like a chimney full of bricks—and have that much behind you, memorable and accomplished—than to be any one of twenty young geniuses breaking out into no matter what art with no matter what talents.'

In this listless and hung-over mood, Jack tried a third marriage.

Since the departure of Clare from his life, his room at the President had become the temporary headquarters for any transient musician who happened by. Often, when he returned from a job in the small hours, he would find the bed and sofa occupied and not wishing to disturb his guests he would sleep in the bathtub, or more often, on the floor. His records were broken or 'borrowed'. And the clothes closet showed evidence of frequent raids. Then, without warning, the room began to take on a civilized appearance. His clothes were laundered and mended, the musicians directed to another room. This improvement continued for some days before he bothered to make inquiries at the desk. The night clerk was asleep in a back room, so he approached the blonde switchboard operator.

'I'd like to find out who's been keeping an eye on my room.'

'I have, Mr. Teagarden,' said the operator. She was Edna 'Billie' Coates, a girl who was possessed of a shrewd business head plus a domineering sense of neatness.

Believing that Jack's inclination towards alcohol diminished following a heavy meal, she encouraged him to eat rich foods. The only effect this had was to increase his weight. With a conscientiousness amounting to fanaticism, Billie set herself to the task of reshaping Jack in her own tidy image. Regarding the cap as a symbol of his frowzy world, she banished it. If Jack sank into any easy chair after a wearying night's work, he would at once find himself the target for Billie's scalp massage, manicure, or even a mud pack. At first mention of the latter, Jack struggled bravely before surrendering. After a while their marriage took on the aspect of a self-improvement course with Jack as an unwilling pupil.

Under Billie's relentless attentions, the welfare and sophisticated appearance of Jack Teagarden seemed assured until one afternoon at their Whitby Arms residence a shattering noise brought Billie rushing to the window. In the street below, surrounded by an admiring crowd and wearing a hoary cap, her husband sat at the wheel of a shining Stanley Steamer. He had just bought it and the purchase revived an affection which was proof against the onslaughts of even Billie's grooming. Chattering at her with small-boy enthusiasm, he pointed out the novelties of the vehicle. A few days later Billie sampled them at closer quarters on a drive south to Texas. It was high summer. Billie's endurance lasted as far as Knoxville, Tennessee, where she decided that she could no longer stand the smell, the heat, nor the comments of passers-by. She alighted and completed the trip by rail.

Jack's passion for steam-engines never diminished, although opportunities for indulgence were scarce. When one came along he made the most of it. Paul Whiteman and Fred Waring had jointly leased rehearsal space in a building at 53rd and Broadway. It was here that the British musicians who played on the *Queen Mary*, then the biggest liner afloat, came in a body to hear their favourite American jazzman. After rehearsal and

THE STORY OF A JAZZ MAVERICK

introductions, he took the British boys on a Manhattan pub-crawl during which he expressed his love for steam machines.

'Come with us,' said his friends, 'and we'll show you the biggest steam job of all.'

Ten hours later Whiteman called Billie. 'I thought he was still with you,' she replied.

'Well, he isn't,' roared Whiteman and summoned a special investigator. Another ten hours elapsed. Finally the missing trombonist was marched into Whiteman's office.

'Found him on the *Queen Mary*,' said the investigator. 'Another hour and she would've sailed.'

Whiteman turned to Jack and snorted. 'You think of all the trouble you caused? You think of me?'

'What a tub, Pops,' Jack replied dreamily. 'What a god-damned tub.'

As his five-year contract drew to a close, Jack felt a tug of loyalty to 'Pops' Whiteman. But it was accompanied by the thrill of impending liberty. Moreover, a vague desire to form and lead his own band now crystallized into a firm intention. Some months earlier an old friend and fellow trombonist handed Jack some arrangements he was peddling about town. 'Ask Paul if he can use them,' he said. Jack brought them to Whiteman's notice.

'No,' said the leader finally. 'They're good, but not for us. Thank him anyway. What's his name?'

'Miller,' said Jack. 'Glenn Miller.'

Now he heard that Miller was forming his own band. Swing was sweeping the country. Gene Krupa and Harry James left Goodman to build their own outfits. Bands were begetting bands. Even Paul Whiteman was unable to totally ignore 'swing' any longer and in the autumn of 1938 he expressed contempt for those who derided it. A popular weekly invited him to select an 'All-American Swing Band'. He included Jack Teagarden and asserted that 'Mr. T. never played an ugly note in his life. He wouldn't know how to'.

As a concession to the trend, Whiteman created a small unit

with Jack as its pivot. He called it the 'Swing Wing' and although its offerings were less passionate than polished, a certain lilting jazz emerged. The old buoyancy crept back into Jack's playing and is particularly displayed on a recording the Wing made of *I'm Coming, Virginia*. But as fresh spirit returned to Jack's performances, so the dream of leading his own band took a stronger hold. He began to talk of the notion between concerts. During intermission at a one-nighter in Lancaster, Pa., before an audience which was described locally as '1,800 alligators and long underwear wearers', he spoke freely of the band he hoped to form. 'On piano will be the finest player of all of them,' he said. 'Peck Kelley.' He added wistfully, 'That is, if he'll leave Texas.''

On Christmas night of 1938, Carnegie Hall was the setting for Paul Whiteman's *Eighth Experiment in Modern Music*. The mighty Whiteman orchestra applied itself while Louis Armstrong, the Raymond Scott Quintette, Walter Gross, Artie Shaw, and the Lyn Murray Singers appeared as guests. It was a long and demanding programme which alternated from Grofe and Gould at their pretentious worst and Gershwin (the *Rhapsody*, of course), to earsplitting exercises in seasonal whimsy. Artie Shaw played the blues ('arranged by Irving Szathmary') and Louis Armstrong sang *Shadrack* with the Lyn Murray Singers. Deems Taylor contributed typically chummy programme notes, in the course of which he observed, 'If, in spite of the fact that you find the music an outrage, the instrumental techniques blasphemous and Mr. Whiteman's taste deplorable —if, despite these calamities, you find yourself having a good time, don't be too resentful. I have an idea that in the days when Haydn and Mozart and Beethoven were grinding out symphonies and concerts and quartets for their princely patrons, about the only question their audiences asked of the music was "is it fun to listen to".' To the disciplined but frustrated Whiteman jazzmen on the stage of Carnegie, to the drummer George Wettling, the trombonist Miff Mole, and to both Teagardens, another question might have been asked—the only question which counts to a pure jazz man. *Is it fun to play?*

That Christmas concert was Jack's last with Paul Whiteman. Snatches of gossip concerning his imminent release from the band were already appearing in the entertainment columns. They were couched in the peculiar journalese of the day. 'There is talk that Jackson Teagarden, the slush pump virtuoso, is planning a small group of his own to include the legendary Peck Kelley, Memphis [*sic*] ivory tickler who has so far refused to leave the confines of a pet beer garden despite offers from big shots.'

The orchestra was playing a matinée at Loew's Theatre. One tune remained to be played in the current set. Jack kept glancing nervously at his watch. When the band had finished the number, Jack carefully wiped off his horn and placed it in the case. Charles watched him curiously.

'Where are you going?' he asked.

Jack stood up. 'Home,' he grinned. 'My five years ran out three minutes ago.'

'We've got another show tonight,' Charles reminded him.

Jack shrugged. 'Miff can play both parts.' He walked towards the door.

Whiteman halted him. 'Jack . . .?'

'I know, Pops. You had plans for me.' He smiled wanly. 'Thanks,' he said. Then he left the theatre and came out into the winter sunshine without a right at all to sing the blues.

Chapter VIII

'THE swing fad,' wrote Wilder Hobson, at the height of it, 'has largely been built on the commercially saleable mixture of a certain amount of jazz playing and a great many compromise, popular melody-and-jazz orchestrations. The jazz is sometimes talented and spirited but it is more likely to be routine or exhibitionistic, with a heavy emphasis on the rhythm-blasting and technical display which delights many audiences.'

The new trend towards more and larger bands provided employment for some (though not all) of the best jazz musicians, bringing them for the first time widespread public notice. A number of swing addicts, once the fad's superficial attractions palled, discovered the deeper joys of jazz. As a result, to the basic instinctive response was added more adult attitudes of contemplation and appreciation. Whatever else it did, the swing craze spotlighted individual jazz musicians and set the stage for the development of mere public notice of jazz into an intelligent public *interest*.

The launching and captaining of an orchestra is a demanding enterprise. Jack Teagarden's business acumen had always been vague. Therefore, his confidence in the presence of his wealthy backer one wintry morning in 1939 was nothing short of remarkable.

John Gluskin waved him to a chair. 'What do you want to get started?'

Jack didn't hesitate. 'My choice of men and arrangements.'

'Get them,' said Gluskin, who was not without a rare optimism himself. 'Get anything else you need. Let's start you off right.'

Jack immediately hired Charlie Spivak, Allen Reuss and Ernie Cacerres, top performers on trumpet, guitar and clarinet. He chose his supporting sidemen with equal discretion. But a sentimental urge clouded his judgment and he hired his brother Cubby to play drums. He could have had no notion of the distress this would cause. Cubby was a youngster, eager to please but lacking in experience and the vital drum position in an ambitious name band was no place for any less than a competent veteran.

While the professional risk of matching strong sidemen with an untried drummer was not apparent to Jack's wife, the proposed salaries made her blink. 'Charlie Spivak's pay cheque will be practically that of a partner,' she complained.

'He's a good man,' Jack said briefly. 'You have to pay good men.'

A management arrangement Jack had entered into with an agent named Arthur Michaud was dissolved, enabling him to sign the band with the Music Corporation of America. The price of release was costly, for he agreed to pay Michaud a sizeable percentage of his gross earnings over a period of three years. It was a hard bargain, but if Jack had no misgivings, Billie had.

Rehearsals were held daily, expenses were rapidly mounting, yet the band's début was nowhere in sight. The situation, Billie felt, called for the intervention of Saint Teresa, her favourite patron. She lit a candle for luck and had no sooner returned from church than the telephone rang. It was Gluskin. 'Good news,' he said. 'The band plays Roseland next Friday. Then it opens at the Terrace Room of the New Yorker.'

'That Teresa,' said Jack when Billie told him,' there's a gal that wastes no time.'

Among those present at the New Yorker opening on April 17th was the critic Irving Kolodin. He wrote, 'Teagarden apparently has no designs on the laurels now held by the bands of the power variety. For the most part the music is subdued with an emphasis on blending and quality rather than blasting, as a background to the remarkable playing of the leader himself.'

Jack sang *I Gotta Right to Sing the Blues*, but nobody had the blues that night. The delight of New York audiences and the praise of the critics were echoed by the good wishes of Jack's colleagues in telegrams which, although typical publicity gestures, strengthened his confidence.

'Swing it, Jack. You have one of the greatest bands in the world'—Benny Goodman.

'Swing into great success'—Tommy Dorsey.

'That terrific band of yours'—Eddy Duchin.

'Hope tonight's opening marks the beginning of a great year'—Harry James.

'Best of luck'—Guy Lombardo.

'Congrats to a swell guy who plays a swell trombone and has a swell band'—Hal Kemp.

More personally sincere was one which read, 'My best wishes. I know you will be a sensation. I just wish I could be with you and come and share in your success. By the way, you'll be an uncle next week—Your loving brother—Charles.'

It would be, as Harry James hoped, a great year for the Jack Teagarden Orchestra. How could it be otherwise? He took the band on a triumphal tour of theatres and everywhere he played the welcome was the same; old friends stepping up to wish him well, new friends and fans clamouring for autographs, columnists pressing for interviews. To one he said, 'I'm well satisfied with the band now. I'm planning no changes. I know we are heading in the right direction.' Jack went on to praise Spivak particularly. But Spivak was destined to remain with him only a short while longer before he too assumed the mantle of big band leadership.

Most outfits employed girl singers, or perhaps more accurately, 'vocalists'. Jack decided a touch of glamour would do the band no harm and conducted a series of auditions. One trim applicant selected *Basin Street Blues* for her number. 'Sorry,' said Jack, who cherished a proprietary affection for the tune. Afterwards he confessed, 'If she'd picked anything else but *Basin Street*, I'd have hired her.' Her name was Dinah Shore.

By the autumn of 1939 it was apparent to Jack that several members of the band would feel happier with a different drummer. 'Nothing against Cubby personally,' they told their leader, 'but this outfit deserves a *great* drummer—someone like Davey Tough.'

To many, Tough was *the* great white jazz drummer. Despite recurrent illness and a restlessness of spirit, seated at his drums the little Chicagoan became a source of rocking power. He would, Jack knew, be good for the band. But as he prepared to hire Tough, he felt a vague tug of disloyalty and postponed telling Cub of his decision. As it happened, this made matters worse. A confusion over dates arose and to Jack's dismay, both his brother and Tough showed up one morning for rehearsal. The two drummers stared at each other. Then they turned to Jack. He tried to frame an explanation but it was no use. The words didn't come. Cub threw a final glance of hurt disbelief at his brother and walked out of the building.

Jack hired Phil Moore as chief arranger for the band. Whenever reference is made to the courage of certain bandleaders in breaking the race barrier, Jack's action is usually ignored. Due tribute is paid to Benny Goodman, Artie Shaw, and a few others for flouting bigotry, but Jack's name is rarely singled out in this respect. An explanation might be found in the fact that the impact of Moore upon the band was slight when compared to that of Sy Oliver on Tommy Dorsey or Fletcher Henderson on Benny Goodman; and most probably, even that isolated precedent in the mid-'twenties when Don Redman not only arranged for but played with the white Paul Specht Orchestra.

Moore is a classically trained musician whose long-cherished dream of a racially integrated music is utterly praiseworthy. Ten years after his work with Teagarden he remarked 'the type of music I am writing practically demands an amalgamation of jazz and classic, Negro and white musicians. This will strengthen the relationship between the classical and jazz musicians who

are fighting a cultural battle. The influence of the Negro
members is needed in the orchestra, the white men are needed,
their combined backgrounds are needed'.

Although he goes on to say that the Boston Symphony could
not play this fancied music, he is speaking of a symphony-sized
orchestra employing standard instrumentation. Moore sees a
future for jazz in technical development and fusion with other
(chiefly European) forms. In the bands of so called 'modernists',
jazz has in fact taken this direction. But its corollary, an emer-
gence of whole jazz-symphonic orchestras with racially-
integrated personnels remains a dream.

Moore was born in Oregon and after his formal training,
worked for radio and film studios in Hollywood. He was never
subjected to jazz influences common to other environments;
and his approach to arranging for large bands was mildly
experimental. His effect upon the Teagarden band was not
vastly different from that of any respectably trained white
arranger.

This middle-of-the-road course, however, failed to pacify
that segment of society which is suspicious of any association
of Negro with white. When Moore accompanied the band on
southern road tours, there occurred nothing more serious than
set-backs in hotel accommodations and similar embarrassments
taken, perhaps too lightly, for granted. But they were enough to
strengthen the belief among bookers, hotel managers, and dance-
hall operators that race mixing, no matter how slight, was bad
for business. This attitude, product of a concern with box-
office receipts, permitted few violations of the unwritten Jim
Crow 'laws'. Benny Goodman's journeys into the South with
Negro musicians were among the boldest steps taken, but even
so their appearances were as a small unit separated from the band.

The truth is that there was no *major* breakthrough in this
sensitive area, and this was due less to lack of spirit on the part
of musicians of both races than to the cravenness of promoters
and bookers. Twenty years later a pusillanimity was still evident. Mixed bands (including one led by Benny Goodman for
the 1958 Brussels Fair) were sent to Europe with the blessings

of a State Department which, however puzzled by the music they played, had apprised it as a means to win foreign friends; or as some bluntly put it, a cold war weapon. No strong zeal was shown back home to send such mixed bands on goodwill tours of the South. They were, it seemed, for export only.

To the despair of those who had hoped that Jack's liberation from Whiteman signified his return as a major jazz force, he displayed no wish to create a jazz-flavoured swing band of the Goodman type and he felt no great urge to crash barriers. Manifest in the ease with which he enjoyed the company of Negroes and the startling unity he was capable of sharing with them in music, was the simple instinct that there *were* no barriers. Only experience and the brusque advice of his commercial investors persuaded him otherwise.

In the belief that Jack's peaks of spontaneous jazz creativity have been reached on those occasions when he worked with Negroes, it may be ventured that no other white leader would have benefited more from their inclusion in his orchestra. They would need to be of approximate stature both in jazz feeling and technical prowess. He had had (and would continue to have) more than his share of mediocrity to work with; mediocre Negroes play no better jazz than mediocre white men. Then, with an élite company, there would be no 'band' and no 'leader'. Just a group of working jazz musicians giving deeper meaning to the word *integration*.

But fame and the novelty of leading a big, commercially successful band were the goals uppermost in Jack's outlook then. Disenchantment had not yet begun to set in. He believed in his band (as he did in every outfit he ever led) and except for an unsuccessful attempt to get Art Tatum into it, he showed no accord with the increasingly disillusioned few who felt that his best jazz was produced when he played with the best Negroes. 'If I'm in the right company, it comes out,' he often said. 'Unless I've got good men around me, I'm no good. There's no inspiration.' But the profit motive is more vital to a big band enterprise than the presence of a jazz quorum. Obedience to social prejudices is a cardinal rule of American business. The association,

then, of an easy-going bandleader with profit-minded business-
men who were either misguidedly cautious or downright in-
competent, was not a promising one. Those who knew Jack
as one of the greatest figures in jazz (even if he himself seemed
unaware of it) now saw him surrounded more and more by
men who, from a jazz standpoint at least, could scarcely be
called 'good company'.

It was the winter of 1939, the time of the safely-distant
European war. The days of America's neutrality might be
numbered, but complacency reigned and the entertainment
world thrived. But Jack was already personally affected by
Hitler's aggressions. 'Everytime we get going,' he complained,
'that guy pulls off another fast one and we're cut off the air for
a news bulletin.' Beyond this, there was little to dampen Jack's
spirits, for the college dates, radio broadcasts, and one-
nighters continued to increase the band's popularity.

He never failed to include a number of outright blues or blue-
tinged pops in his performances and was billed as 'The Man
with the Blue Trombone plus his Band—Sixteen Men and a
Girl'. The girl was Kitty Kallen, an attractive singer with a
natural flair for ballads. One desperately whimsical booker
advertised them as 'Sixteen Tea Leaves and a Lump of Sugar'.

Kitty left the band suddenly after marrying a Teagarden
sideman and was replaced by Marianne Dunn out of Horace
Heidt's talent show. Miss Dunn's singing experience had been
chiefly confined to children's parties in her Akron, Ohio home.
The jump from parlour to network broadcasts was abrupt and
during her first show with the band Miss Dunn's nerves
collapsed. Happily she recovered, dropped the Dunn from her
name, and assumed the haughty glamour expected of a name
band vocalist. She stayed with the band long enough to record
I Hear Bluebirds, one of a number of unexciting records the
band cut for the Varsity label.

Early the next year Jack was brusquely informed that he
owed Arthur Michaud $4,500. He disputed the amount and
Michaud promptly complained to the American Federation of

Musicians. The union's response was rude and swift. 'Better pay up,' Jack was told; if he didn't, his union card would be seized.

He turned to Gluskin for help. 'Look,' the man said, 'I gave you a free band. What more can I do?'

'Every cent I've drawn on the road went for expenses,' Jack pleaded. Gluskin shrugged and withdrew his interest. On the advice of his attorney, Andrew Weinberger, Jack filed a petition for bankruptcy. The A.F.M. announced that it didn't recognize bankruptcy. The complexities of the impending legal showdown were outside Jack's comprehension but he shivered upon hearing that the necessary steps to seize his card were being taken. They were halted when Weinberger successfully sought a temporary injunction to restrain the union from forcing a settlement. As the U.S. District Court referee stated, 'The laws of the United States are superior to the rules and regulations of the A.F.M.' He set March 28th as the day for the hearing. Until then, at least, Jack's card was safe.

His refusal to yield without a struggle was studied with interest and admiration. 'It took guts to fight the A.F.M. as Teagarden did,' said *Downbeat*. 'Even now he faces the loss of his livelihood.' But after a thoughtful couple of months, the A.F.M., unwilling to risk an unfavourable decision in an unprecedented court action, agreed to a private settlement. Michaud was satisfied and thus ended an interesting test case for working musicians everywhere.

Having tilted his lance, so to speak, at union bureaucracy, Jack reorganized his band on a less ambitious scale and confessed, 'I've learned my lesson. There are two ways to get a band started—the *de luxe* way and the right way. This year we're going at it the right way even if it's the hard way.'

Not everybody thought it was the right way. One critic wrote, 'Teagarden's new organization includes seven brass, five saxes, drums, bass, and piano. The brass section is an ear-blaster. The new band may not play the best swing but they certainly play the loudest.'

By mid-May the band had played at thirty-eight college dates.

Sometimes, on the day following the dance, a campus lecture was delivered on the nature and function of steam engines by the distinguished authority, Mr. Jack Teagarden. During the University of Toledo spring prom, Jack announced a novelty called *A Chicken ain't Nothin' but a Bird*. He did so with a brave smile and a faint stirring of distaste. This was not what he had bargained for. But the crowds applauded *A Chicken* as they did *Fatima's Drummer Boy, I've Got a Hat with Cherries* and similar grotesques. The stuff was as alien to him as the old Whiteman 'symphonic jazz' had been. But brassy novelty seemed to be what the masses wanted, and if there were two ways to start a band, there was only one way to keep it going— the popular way. In a sense, Jack felt he was now more a prisoner than he had been in his Whiteman days. The applause he got at Toledo University held more authority than Paul's baton. It brought home to him what Glenn Miller and Benny Goodman had already learned. You might be leader of the band but the public was boss.

The boss could be generous. Jack's new band prospered. It broadcast five nights a week, played the more fashionable resorts, and attended society shindigs. Despite the roar of artillery fire from a near-by National Guard camp, it enjoyed a pleasant summer at Seagirt Inn, New Jersey.

And with his attractive smile and sleek black hair, Jack was one of the most photogenic of the popular bandleaders. He voiced no objections when these attributes were used for advertisements for tooth-paste and a 'Free Scalp Analysis'.

At a Wardman Park dance in Washington, D.C., someone requested a conga. Jack obliged. 'Just like Cugat,' yelled an overcome lady. At once the well-dressed mob forced the band into a Latin-American rut from which they escaped only when refreshments were served. Then, for a heavenly handful of minutes, the band played *St. James Infirmary*.

With Paul Wimbish as manager, the Teagarden Orchestra continued to follow the high society party line. Playing waltzes for a débutants' coming-out party held at the Connecticut Hunt Club, its presence was duly noted by the local gossip scrivener.

'Mrs. Palmer's outfit was a black lace skirt and a pink taffetta jacket. Summer flowers decorated the clubhouse. Jack Teagarden played for dancing.'

A Baltimore night-club operator told Jack, 'You've got a great band. You keep 'em listening, not dancing. And the more they sit and listen, the more drinks we sell. Yes, sir, you've got a great band.'

The Baltimore customers were undoubtedly not youthful. Otherwise, not even Jack Teagarden's band could have kept them off the dance floor. For this was the era of the jitterbug whose whirling gyrations were far more energetic than the rock-'n'-rollers of a later generation. Jack accepted an invitation to play at the Norfolk City Auditorium. The authorities, despite his gentle title of 'The Troubador of the Blue Trombone', feared that his band might spark jitterbugs to such a degree the old building would be imperilled. As a safety precaution the event was altered from a dance to a concert. It made no difference. One week after the affair the auditorium was totally condemned. At his next stop, Jack was described as 'Stonewall Jackson Teagarden', an ironic tag considering how non-aggressive his trombone playing had become.

The alliance of Jack's natural carelessness with plain bad luck began a sniping campaign. Separated from the band one weekend, he arranged to meet it for a concert at Greenville, North Carolina. He got into town at four in the afternoon, ample time, he told himself, to get some rest before the show. It wasn't until he switched on the radio in his hotel room that he learned he was in Greenville, South Carolina. He dashed to the lobby to be told there was no regular plane service to North Carolina that night. 'Any chance of a charter?' he asked.

'We'll fly you for fifty-seven fifty if you'll navigate.'

They took off in cloudy weather, skipped over a couple of heavy squalls, and were trapped in the middle of a third. Just then the pilot discovered he was low on petrol. He hurried out of the storm, landed bumpily at Fort Bragg and asked the U.S. Army for fuel. 'This is Jack Teagarden,' he said. 'In two hours he opens at Greenville.'

'North Carolina,' Jack added.

'Too bad,' said the Army. 'We can't let you off the ground in this weather.'

'How far is it to Greenville?' asked Jack. 'North Carolina?'

'One hundred and twenty miles.'

Surrounded by sympathetic soldiers, Jack stood in the wind and rain and groaned. Then a sergeant spoke up. 'I'll take you there on my motor-cycle,' he offered. 'I collect all your records.'

'Thanks,' said Jack, 'but I'd better take a taxi.' He hired a cab with a driver who stammered badly. It took the driver several minutes to explain why he was making a wide detour through Fayetteville to pick up his wife.

'A-a hun-hun-dred m-m-m-miles is a l-long t-t-t-trip. I'll n-need c-c-company on the way h-h-h-home.' It was nearly midnight when Jack unpacked his horn in the right Greenville and led the band without conviction through *The World is Waiting for the Sunrise*.

On another occasion he emplaned for South Bend to play at a benefit and was the only one present informally attired. 'Damn' well won't happen again,' he growled. The next day he joined the band in Bloomington for a college prom. This time he climbed on the stand, smiling and impeccably clad in his tuxedo. His smile vanished. Nobody had briefed him that this was the first informal dance of the season.

And there were accommodation difficulties. In Washington, D.C. one week-end, Jack and his musicians battled with Cherry Blossom Festival tourists for room space. Two weeks later they were back in Washington to find the hotels even more thoroughly occupied by the Daughters of the American Revolution. They went on to Raleigh and fought hordes of fans who had swept into town for the All-State High School Basketball Finals. Charleston, Charlotte and Birmingham were all jammed with conventions.

'Now I know what southern hospitality means,' said Seymour Goldfinger, Jack's second trombonist, one morning as he wearily rubbed his back. 'They have the widest park benches down here.'

Benny Goodman

Eddie Condon

Compensation for such physical discomforts, common to all travelling dance bands, was often provided by the variegated company they met while on tour. At the Roxy, in Atlantic City, Jack shared the billing with a team of dancing puppets; he played before, after, and briefly and inadvertently during, a juvenile crime prevention forum held at the Oriental Beach bandshell in Brooklyn. Under the chairmanship of the MacNeil of Barra, and attended by all the Scotsmen in New York City, a benefit for the British Ambulance Corps was organized in the Waldorf Astoria. Jack's band joined the forty-man bagpipe team from Scotland. Fraternization developed among the musicians and took the form of Jack and the trumpeter Johnny Fallstitch blowing a few un-Gaelic patterns around *The Wee Macgregor* while the pipes carried the theme. This so delighted the musicians, both kilted and tuxedoed, that talk of an all-in cutting contest followed. It was hastily squashed by the MacNeil.

Jack was now giving the public what it seemed to like best: noisy novelties (*Chicks is Wonderful*), alternating with dreamy, danceable pops (*The Moon and the Willow Tree*). It was a profitable formula although it dismayed those who considered him valuable only as an untrammelled jazz artist. Here was yet another example, they felt, of a development familiar in every art—the sacrifice of principle for the achievement of commercial success. A natural impression, but not wholly valid. For one thing, few if any of this era's best jazzmen paused to regard their music as 'art'; certainly they exhibited none of the lofty self-consciousness all too common in later decades.

This is not to say that jazz is not art; as a deeply personal, highly spontaneous mode of expression it doubtless qualifies. But the musicians did not think so—or say so—until persuaded to by articulate critics who quite properly rescued the music from its artificial context of jive jargon, jitterbugs, and commercial exploitation; simultaneously defended it against the derision of 'classical music' snobs; and dignified it with the word 'art'. By the nineteen-fifties these worthy efforts had produced an unfortunate side effect; a large number of more or less talented youngsters talked soberly and interminably in magazine interviews or on record album sleeves of what their artistic aims were, while their proven peers suffered a silent embarrassment or offered laconic comment and never for a moment deserted the belief that in jazz, the music must speak for itself.

No notion crossed Jack's mind that he was 'prostituting his art'. In any event, the refinement of his trombone work in the nineteen-forties was nothing suddenly new, but had been obviously acquired during the long years with Whiteman. This smoothed yet unmistakably blue-tinged tone seemed to be to the crowd's liking. It never occurred to him to change it. Furthermore, he was a bandleader now and shouldered a responsibility which, in contrast to the jazz-is-an-art argument, was perfectly clear. His prime duty, as he saw it, was to maintain steady and remunerative employment for his musicians. How successfully he discharged it could only be measured by public response.

Those who had followed Jack's career since the Harlem days were not pleased. The jazz quality in his horn had been weakened, first by the Pollack-Foyer excesses, then by the heavy handed polishing of Whiteman. Listening to his records would confirm this. His present activities could only result in further dilution. But those who thought this were among the apostles of the jazz-is-an-art faith, a minority group reviled or ridiculed, not yet able to describe its own tenets coherently, and whose devotion to a jazz musician, however heartwarming, could seldom guarantee his livelihood.

The change in Jack's tone had been a very gradual one. He was not unaware of it but in no way regarded it as deterioration. He often shuddered at the material which the public seemed to prefer, and sought compensation in the blues. He could not help but do so. The blues feeling is such an integral part of his musical nature that nothing could have erased it. Conveyed through the trombone, it ceases to be a mere personal complaint, but is strengthened by defiance, made beautiful by wistfulness, and achieves structural grandeur from his technical prowess. Ill-defined and still controversial in its origins, the blues is the most potent raw material of jazz. Even those pessimistic viewers with alarm of Jack's decline gained some comfort from the occasional evidence he gave of his continuing pre-eminence among white musicians in the fashioning of the blues; reminders of why he is numbered among the few great architects of this music.

It is impossible for him to keep the blues out of his playing. Therefore, during his period of popular success as a band-leader, his programmes included such titles as *Aunt Hagar's Blues, St. James Infirmary Blues, Muddy River Blues,* and *Basin Street.* But whether twelve bar traditionals, sixteen bar comedy songs, or thirty-two bar sentimental pops, blue inflexions were present in the playing of the leader and sometimes, though not often enough, in the *sound* of the Teagarden-influenced band. Then, the blue treatment of otherwise flimsy tunes made it that much more pleasurable to play them and did not, Jack was happy to note, dismay audiences.

But as the summer of 1940 wore on, the band entertained at society functions so frequently that even Dorothy Kilgallen was moved to write, 'I remember when Teagarden grabbed a trombone and played pure blue notes into the fast air of the 'twenties. Now they're billing him as a débutante bandleader, a stick-wielder for vacationing tourists. It kills me. . . .'

Not with the precise aim of reassuring Miss Kilgallen, Jack made a series of recordings that same month with Bud Freeman, Eddie Condon, Pee Wee Russell, and others of the New York-Chicago gang. After the rigid routine of the band business, the reunion was a tonic Jack was anxious to taste. In the studio, awaiting the arrival of trumpeter Max Kaminsky, he suddenly said, 'Let's knock one off for the hell of it.' Without delay or a trumpet they dug into a blues, throughout which Jack blew a number of 'pure blue notes' and sang twelve bars to boot.

When Kaminsky showed up, they were listening to the play-back. 'Maybe I should come late all the time,' he said. They finished the date with *That Da Da Strain* and *Prince of Wails.* Then Jack returned to the band, another tour, and more broadcasts.

One morning Paul Wimbish showed him a clipping from the *Baltimore Sun*. 'Last evening,' said the writer, 'I listened first to John L. Lewis. Then I listened to Count Basie. Then I listened to Jack Teagarden. Then I listened to Wendell Wilkie. The impression made on me first was that I had been present at a sort of American phantasmagoria and, second, that there is no place like America.'

'What's a phantasmagoria?' asked Jack.

Wimbush shrugged. 'With Wilkie and those others in here, it can't be bad.'

'Unless some Democrat wrote it,' said Jack thoughtfully.

That night, Billie folded her newspaper and said, 'Listen to *this*.'

Jack was repairing an alarm clock but he listened patiently as Billie read that Hollywood was planning a new Bing Crosby film, a jazz story which would require a good band.

'Now if an old friend of Bing's called him,' said Billie, 'and that old friend just happened to have a successful band, and . . .'

'I know what you're hinting,' said Jack.

'Fine. What are you waiting for?'

'No. If they want me they'll call.'

The film studios had tried to reach him already. Unknown to the Teagardens, they had phoned various restaurants and clubs, each time leaving messages for Jack to call back. He hadn't done so because of his old aversion to telephones.

In April 1941 he arrived in Hollywood and the band opened at the Casa Manana. The club swarmed with stars, among whom Lana Turner, Tony Martin, Walter Abel and Deanna Durbin saw fit to leave their tables to offer words of encouragement to the bandleader.

'Thanks,' he told them, 'but I don't have a speaking part. I just play my horn.' This suited Jack, but not Billie.

'You could handle a bigger role,' she said.

'How about Bing's?' he suggested, 'or Mary Martin's?'

She ignored his sarcasm as she invariably did on the rare occasions when he indulged in it. 'They need someone to play

"Pepper". Allen Jenkins is being considered but I don't think he's keen.'

Next day Jack went along to the lot and read 'Pepper's' script. When he got back that night, Billie told him, 'I prayed to Saint Teresa that you'd get the part.'

'That's some chick,' Jack said. 'You'd better go back to church and thank her.' He chuckled. 'Say "Pepper" sent you.'

It was a pleasure to be with Bing again. Since the old days at the Belvedere, Bing's progress in show business had been phenomenal. He had remained, however, the lover of good fun and a relaxed life that Jack had known over ten years before. And his love for Jack's brand of jazz was as boundless as ever. In later years he voiced his opinion of the trombonist with the words, 'I yield to no man in my unbounded admiration for his talents, his abilities, and his wonderful good taste.'

Both men enjoyed working together. But Jack's efforts as a serious actor were hampered by Wingy Manone who, though not in the cast, hung around sabotaging the trombonist's scenes with various mischiefs. Despite Wingy, *Birth of the Blues* turned out to be an entertaining movie, fondly remembered for *The Waiter, the Porter, and the Upstairs Maid* sung lustily by Bing, Jack, and Mary Martin.

By the time the film was finished, Billie felt homesick. Moreover, Jack's entry into film circles had attracted a horde of fresh admirers and, as usual, indiscretions occurred which, though mild, found Billie less patient and forgiving than her predecessors. She packed her bags and returned to New York. The rift was sudden and for Jack, at least, unforeseen. He was left with the familiar feeling of hurt surprise, only this time the reaction was briefer. It vanished before the advent of a letter from Vernon asking him to pay a visit.

He had often wondered about the attitude of the citizens of Vernon to his career in jazz music. His memories of the town were hazy now. Band tours had never taken him sufficiently near for a call. His old friends, however, had not forgotten him and his plans and accomplishments had been faithfully recorded by the local press.

Another ex-pupil of old Paul Goetze had also achieved eminence in the music world. Cathy Pierce, young Weldon's childhood sweetheart, now played a violin in the Houston Symphony Orchestra. It was Cathy who proposed to the Junior Chamber of Commerce that it invite Vernon's most famous celebrity to appear there after an absence of twenty years.

Jack accepted at once and insisted that any profits from the visit should go to the Vernon Nursery School. Cathy Pierce aided plans for a civic reception and on a sultry day in 1941 the Teagarden Orchestra was met east of town at Paradise Creek by a caravan of siren-equipped cars. Noisily the parade moved into Vernon beneath huge banners bearing the greeting, WELCOME HOME WELDON JACK.

'Who the hell is Weldon Jack?' one of the newer members of the band asked clarinettist Danny Polo.

'Your boss, sonny,' replied Polo. 'Who else?'

The bandleader was escorted to the Town Hall where the Mayor of Vernon announced, 'I do proclaim Tuesday, August 12th, as Teagarden Day and urge all to participate in the activities designed to honour a native son,' after which he presented Jack with the key to the city. Helen Teagarden, who had journeyed from Oklahoma City for the occasion, stood in tearful pride beside her son on the Town Hall steps. The citizens and honoured guests then adjourned to a giant barbecue where the tables were arranged to form a letter 'T'.

Before dressing for the nursery benefit dance, Jack escaped the crowd to wander around the scene of his childhood. He had been drinking and fell easily into a nostalgic mood. Memories gathered, some sad, some hazily happy; of his father worriedly struggling with the cornet; of toy oil derricks in the backyard; of Pendleton's drug store and the Court House concerts. The images faded before darker thoughts of the band business scramble, of Billie and women in general and of the schoolboy love of engineering which had grown with him and was now never appeased. And of the conviction (which rarely left him) that whatever he said in music, he could have expressed better. His reverie was interrupted by Cathy Pierce and Danny

Polo who had been searching for him. They found him leaning on the fence near the railway tracks at the bottom of Mesquite Street.

That night the band played (sometimes accompanying Miss Pierce for violin solos) to the biggest crowd Hill Crest Country Club had ever seen. Everybody sweltered despite the portable cooling system—specially rented for the event—and the invitation to the guests to 'wear anything comfortable from playsuits to evening clothes'. The heat forced them and the band out on to the floodlit tennis court where a number of local persons sang their tributes, after which Vernon's native son and his nineteen musicians applauded energetically.

Next day the band moved on and elder citizens of the town told each other the place had never seemed so quiet.

The rancour of his parting from Billie precluded any reconciliation; with a third marriage behind him, he was in no hurry to tackle a fourth. Women, he assured himself, were all very well, but a man could get along without them. He couldn't help feeling discouraged by the swiftness with which this conviction fled whenever confronted by a fair face or figure. Then, unprotected, he shrugged and let matters take care of themselves. His attitude to his band was similarly careless—not in affairs of music, where his judgment firmly ruled, but in the adjacent realm of business.

A bandleader is usually required to concern himself with music, leaving accountancy and road management to others. But it is to everyone's interest that he at least comprehend these matters, for should things go awry, the responsibility will surely be laid at his door, a truism applying to other fields of endeavour as well. To Jack's credit, he made a couple of serious attempts to check the band's ledgers but each time the figures defeated him. There were occasions when they defeated his accountants, too.

Perhaps the most competent management which the band enjoyed was exercised by Charles Boulanger, a friendly fellow with a keen sense of business matters and a rapidly formed knack of coping with the hourly dilemmas of dance-band control.

During a fortnight's job at the Meadowbrook Country Club in St. Louis, Jack fell in love with an aviatrix. Boulanger was sufficiently acquainted with the leader's past sorties in romance to know their capacity for producing even more dilemmas. But this one, he hoped, might work out differently since it was he who had drawn the pair together. The meeting took place at Lambert Field where Boulanger had a couple of friends. One of them was a vivacious divorcee named Adeline Barriere, who possessed somewhat more flamboyance than Jack was accustomed to and an indefatigable good humour which conquered him at once.

Addie did not capitulate to Jack's charms quite so promptly. But a series of romantic flights shared in a Piper Cub which she piloted, left her in no doubt that she too was in love. When the Meadowbrook job ended and the Piper Cub descended for the last time, Jack said good-bye with more reluctance than he had ever felt before.

In 1941 he appeared on a magazine cover dressed as a trombone-playing Father Time. A scantily clad calendar girl stood beside him asking, 'What's in store for 1942, Jack?' The magazine reached the stands a couple of days before the band opened at the Hotel Sherman in Chicago. No one could have foreseen that the cover picture proved less a publicity stunt than a grim omen, for the Japs chose the same day to play a noisier opening at Pearl Harbour.

The entertainment profession was no more prepared for the conflict than were the military forces. But in America, more than anywhere, show business is a potent industry. Its publicists soon assured the nation that neither the combat soldier nor the defence plant worker could function satisfactorily without entertainment. Ample evidence supported the claim and Congress unhesitatingly appropriated first half a million dollars and then an additional eight hundred thousand for the newly formed United Services Organization, which, in return, furnished entertainment ranging from name bands and movie stars to jugglers, singers and vaudeville comics not heard from since the Depression.

'Music can help win this war,' cried *Downbeat* and went on to cite President Roosevelt's opinion that there should be more bands and more parades. *Downbeat* went further—the bands should also play in army camps and defence plants where the war effort could be spurred by 'pulse-racing, patriotic music'.

It is open to question whether America's pulses raced any more rapidly to *God Bless America* than to the *Two o'Clock Jump*. But *Downbeat* was on the right track by pushing music as a morale booster. It was only a matter of time before such journals were urging that, in order to keep musicians in action and morale-boosting at maximum pitch, transportation restrictions and the demands of the draft should be relaxed. This call was not heeded.

In August of that year, James C. Petrillo clamped the lid on the phonograph recording business. In an attempt to protect his musicians from 'the musical monsters which were killing employment', he forbade all recording activities. U.S. troops were already being sent to countless overseas bases, and as though to bolster the pleas of *Downbeat* for more music, letters poured back home demanding records. The Army, well aware of the effect of music on morale hastily formulated a plan to initiate, produce, and distribute recordings of 'name' musicians and entertainers. Caught up by the war spirit, no doubt, Petrillo issued permission for his musicians to record for the Army with no remuneration to the individuals concerned and accompanied by a waiver of publisher's and composer's royalties. Following this generous example, the major recording companies (with the exception of Decca) donated their entire master libraries to the programme.

Thus the V-Disc label, which was to nurture an enormous wealth of original jazz sessions, was born. Unhampered by the sometimes rigid musical standards of commercial recording concerns, unorthodox personnel and arrangements were commonplace and the resulting records produced some of the finest jazz ever documented. Teagarden contributed tirelessly in consort with 'Lips' Page, Armstrong, Bobby Hackett, Lou McGarrity and other men of comparable stature; *Jack-Armstrong*

Blues, The Sheik of Araby, and *Miss Martingale* were
a few of the matchless sides cut by these oddly-assorted groups.
Sadly, none of these recordings were ever released commercially because of the donation of the musicians' services. After
the war the masters were destroyed and a valuable segment of
American jazz history lost forever.

The draft, of course, mauled bands so severely that they soon
lost their pre-Pearl Harbour identity. Personnels changed so
rapidly it became difficult for a bandleader to name his men
correctly at any given moment. At Jack's persuasion, his sister
Norma joined the band as pianist. 'There's one musician the
draft won't touch,' he said. Next day he lost his brass section
and half his reeds to the Air Corps. Doggedly he replaced them
but he still lacked a strong trumpet player.

While still at the Sherman, Jack heard Jimmy McPartland
was in town. He tracked the trumpeter down at once and made
an offer. At first McPartland hesitated. He'd been beset by
personal troubles and he hadn't worked much lately except for
scattered jobs with mediocre locals. Maybe his technique had
suffered. Jack heard his excuses in silence, then said, 'Do I have
to *draft* you?'

'But you haven't heard me play in thirteen years.'

'That's right,' said Jack, 'Seems like yesterday, doesn't it?'

A few days later at the Firemen's Ball in Louisville, Jimmy
McPartland unsheathed his horn and blew right back into Jack's
life. He left it shortly after he ate the grasshoppers. Never the
type to bandy words over a point, the Chicago trumpeter
prefers to illustrate it. He got involved in a discussion
concerning the wartime food shortage.

'Things might get worse,' said Jimmy. 'We should learn to
live off the land.' They were driving across barren countryside,
Addie at the wheel.

'How could anybody live off the land out here?' she scoffed.

'Stop the car,' McPartland ordered. He got out, snatched a
grasshopper in flight and bit off its head. All about them were
grasshoppers. 'Food,' said McPartland, 'every one of them.'

'Think things will ever get that tough?' asked Jack with

interest. Addie paled, invited McPartland in and hastily drove off. Some days later McPartland entered the Army and was sent to England where even the grasshoppers were rationed.

The band business was approaching frenzy. The recording ban deprived many musicians of a good portion of their income; the rubber scarcity and consequent tyre shortage worried road managers to the brink of nervous breakdowns. In vain did Petrillo plead for concessions on behalf of the travelling musician. Military personnel, naturally, had priority in all areas of transportation while the entertainers were forced to travel the best way they could. Band buses became an even scarcer luxury. The railways could be used, of course, but dance bands by virtue of their size and equipment were at a disadvantage. Air travel was out of the question except in cases where the Army put a plane at a band's disposal. Such acts of generosity, by no means common, might be subject to a number of exigencies from military requirements to a commanding officer's attitude towards swing music.

Once Jack and the band landed at a Louisiana base in a C-47. The aircraft taxied to a position in front of several hundred troops who presented arms smartly. A knot of staff officers strode up. Jack, first to deplane, doffed his cap. 'Sure nice of you boys to give us such a welcome.'

As the others climbed out and unloaded their instruments, the commanding officer turned crimson, hissed at his aides, who hastily dismissed the now grinning troops.

That night at the officers' club the C.O. turned to his adjutant. '*So*, you got the dates mixed up. What two-star general plays music like this?'

Later in the year the band effort was hit by two more blows; petrol rationing and the 'freezing' of special trains. Meanwhile the draft continued to eat into personnel. In the face of these trials, some units simply dissolved. A few, like the Bob Crosby band, enlisted *en masse*. Others scrambled for 'safe' jobs on radio or in hotels where the problems of transportation were minor or non-existent.

Weakened by the vicissitudes of war on the home front, the

profession was also undermined by scandal. At the height of the swing craze some of its top figures had performed in an unwarranted glare of publicity. The notoriety which surrounded the marijuana smoking of a few was similarly out of proportion to the magnitude of the offence and the rank of the offenders. But inevitably it threw the whole popular music field in an ugly light and led certain Congressmen to denounce, with more heat than knowledge, 'jitterbug' music and musicians. Bandleaders already had their hands full but some, including the Dorsey brothers and Harry James, replied to the attack by signing a petition of protest.

Hampered by transport problems, harassed by personal (as well as personnel) distractions, without the publicity of scandal or protest, indeed without any publicity at all, Jack and his band drove into an intensive campaign of army camp shows which few other organizations even equalled. This was no burning drive of patriotism, but a simple sense of dedication which his 3-A draft status had not frustrated. Charles had joined the Air Corps and was last heard from blowing reveille in the Azores, while Jack Jr. was somewhere in the Pacific.

'Hell,' Jack said to Boulanger one night in a Cincinnati bar, 'I'm going to enlist.'

Despite the tired protests of his manager, he got up, swayed slightly, then walked with a decided list down the street where a large model ship served as a recruiting station. 'I'm coming aboard,' he shouted.

The recruiting sergeant recognized him. 'You're already aboard,' he replied, 'so long as you keep playing,' and sent him back to Boulanger.

The Teagarden band was aboard, all right. By automobile until the tires wore out and vehicles sometimes overturned on icy roads, by crowded train or army plane, the band crossed and recrossed the nation playing camp after camp, night after night, its route spinning a vast coast-to-coast web on the national map.

To keep at all solvent, Jack had to squeeze in an occasional commercial date but most of the time the ratio was nine service shows to one civilian affair. From Fort Jay, Governor's Island, to the Armoury at Fort Sumter, before Seabees in San Jose and amputees in a Spokane army hospital, the band played and Jack sang and their rewards, though little more than the thanks of generals and cheers of G.I.s, could never be measured in terms of material profit.

Unfortunately, a band's overhead demands profit and this in turn depends upon public notice. In subordinating his needs to those of the Army, Jack sacrificed the lucrative attention of the fans. In late 1942, while he was working harder than ever before, his band was not mentioned anywhere in *Downbeat*'s annual poll.

No matter how significant they might be, popularity polls were not weighing on Jack's mind. In the midst of a particularly stormy tour, Charles Boulanger's parents suffered simultaneous strokes. Jack, ready for any excuse which would bring Addie to his side, called her in St. Louis.

'There's something I want to ask you. . . .' He hesitated and at the other end of the line Addie smiled. Although they had decided to stay apart until his divorce from Billie was final, it wasn't necessary, she felt, for him to propose a second time. But it would be nice to hear.

'Will you . . .?' he began.

'Will I what?' she encouraged.

'Will you be my band manager?'

Boulanger grinned and took the phone from Jack. 'It won't be for long, Addie. I'll be back. You'll be all right as long as you don't take any lip from anyone.'

She arrived the following day and accepted the books and payroll gravely. Despite her realistic attitude towards life, Addie was not without a streak of sentiment and considered the management of Jack's band a solemn charge; she always would, although much of the time she would have described it simply as 'murder'.

Boulanger didn't come back. Addie kept the job until one summer afternoon she collapsed in a Shreveport hotel. Doctors advised surgery. She was in no shape to make decisions and when he heard of her plight, neither was Jack. He accompanied her to the hospital from where he telephoned her mother in St. Louis.

'Come down here right away,' he urged. 'Addie is . . . Addie . . . well, she's in the hospital. You'd better come down here.' Then he hung up and hurried to Addie's bedside.

In St. Louis, her mother was wondering where 'down here' was. The operator traced the call to Shreveport, hospitals were checked, and in a matter of hours the mother arrived.

The following September, in Sioux Falls, Jack took his band manager to be his lawful wedded wife.

The military itinerary of the Teagarden band was so comprehensive that reunions with familiar faces and places were happily common. A concert for the G.I.s at Fort Sill revived Jack's memories of the end of the other war when he played in the doughboys' band. A dance at Brooks Field, San Antonio, conjured an image of the half-forgotten memories of the old Horn Palace, now long vanished. On to Kelly Field where Jack played for Air Corps youngsters who had never savoured Mrs. Shand's pies. Seven shows in seven days boosted the morale of the sailors around Norfolk, and at the eighth show Terry Shand came up and pumped Jack's hand. Then he sat in at the piano and the reunion lasted all night and saddled both with the largest hangover since their tequila experiment of twenty years before.

The hazards of wartime band travel, while not always dire, were varied. Before setting out on a railroad jaunt from Washington, D.C., to Miami, Addie had the library, music stands and props tagged and safely piled on a baggage truck. Then she ushered the band aboard, a sometimes painful job requiring sudden interruption of farewell embraces. She climbed after the bandsmen as the train moved off.

Norma looked out of the window. She nudged Addie. 'Steel yourself, sister,' she said. 'I think they're loading our stuff on the wrong train.' They were. Next day the band played two army dances and a network Coca-Cola show without music.

In late 1943 while playing the theatre circuit in Texas, Jack suffered from ptomaine poisoning. Addie was visiting her mother in St. Louis. When she learned of her husband's illness she telephoned immediately and got the same start Clare had had ten years before. It wasn't Patsy this time, but a Texas well-wisher whom Jack hastily tried to pass off as his nurse. 'She's taking good care of me, too,' he added.

'I'll bet,' snapped Addie and slammed the phone down.

The incident was just another squall in the often stormy early days of Jack's fourth marriage. It sometimes took an inner strength which Addie never knew she possessed to control herself and preserve her humour. She was often helped by some advice Louis Armstrong once gave her on extra-marital activities: 'Know what I always tell my Lucille?' he had said. 'Pay no mind to all them chippies, honey. You just remember you my one an' only missus.'

To lay a cornerstone for what they hoped would be a lasting marriage, the Teagardens bought a home on the fringe of Long Beach. 'I don't suppose we'll move in until after the war,' Jack guessed. They moved in a week later when a fresh assault by the draft board had crippled the band. Frank Horrington, the drummer, registered at a near-by hotel to serve as an unofficial contractor for Jack whenever a job arose. It was customary then for jobless musicians on the west coast to stroll daily the length of Vine Street, for here deals were made, work found. Horrington ran into Joe Sullivan one day. Joe had been playing solo piano at the Hangover Club in San Francisco. As a result of the meeting, Jack and Sullivan played a series of dates along the coast.

During intermission one evening, the Teagardens were joined by a persuasive extrovert who, unwittingly or not, was destined to write finish to Jack's career as a big bandleader. He spoke of his excellent references, his valuable experience as a band manager, his knowledge of law and book-keeping. He so effectively described his qualifications that even Addie's characteristic caution was deceived. They had been on the look-out for a manager to relieve some of her burden. George

Chumas, according to George Chumas, was just the man they were seeking.

The band re-formed and went out on a nation-wide tour. Chumas took over almost immediately. In fact, so jealously did he guard his control that not only was Addie's interest challenged but it seemed to arouse in him a bitter resentment. Within a few weeks the executive branch of the Teagarden band became a trinity of mistrust. Innuendoes and whispered complaints were exchanged, always over innumerable bottles of liquor.

Fortunately, this uneasiness did not affect the band. As with his previous organization, Jack pegged away at the army camps and air bases with only infrequent interruptions for the more remunerative appearances at theatres or hotels. This policy, however cheering to countless servicemen, failed to keep the band afloat longer than a year.

But the jazz critics' poll of the serviceman's most popular magazine certainly reflected their own appreciation of the trombonist. *Esquire*'s wartime career is chiefly recalled as a valuable source of Quonset Hut pin-ups but it also pioneered in jazz journalism, bringing to it a fresh maturity in contrast to the flippancy, scorn or downright ignorance with which other non-trade organs approached the music. Among the useful contributions which resulted from *Esquire*'s interest, despite the frictional hazards under which the magazine's bipartisan jazz panel seemed constantly to live, was the annual poll.

In the trombone category, Jack's name received the highest rating. Accordingly, in January of 1944, he played in the *Esquire* Jazz Concert held at the Metropolitan Opera House. Without question he was in good company. Louis Armstrong Roy Eldridge, Coleman Hawkins, Barney Bigard, Art Tatum, Sid Catlett, Al Casey, Oscar Pettiford, Lionel Hampton, Red Norvo and Mildred Baily, with Billie Holiday singing arias never before heard in this building. The concert was recorded, and issued only on an ill-fated V-Disc. Jack's singing and playing at this concert only emphasized his creative ability when surrounded by the 'right' men.

Chris Barber and his band welcome Jack Teagarden and Earl Hines at London Airport

Jack Teagarden putting the Royal Cambodian Orchestra on to tape

By January 1945, Jack was back in Hollywood making sound effects for a pair of Universal-International cartoons entitled *The Sliphorn King of Polaroo* and *The Pied Piper of Basin Street*. He was seen as well as heard in *Twilight on the Prairie*, but as this was a grade 'B' quickie, featuring Johnny Downs, it did nothing to restore Jack's popularity. He was invited to appear at a much-touted jam session to announce Horace Heidt's opening at the Trianon, Los Angeles, but all this produced was a clamour of sour notes when Heidt complained that his guests had been overpayed.

Even Jack knew by now that he had lost public acclaim entertaining the military; faulty management, plain bad luck, mediocre sidemen, any or all of these could be blamed for his five failures as a big bandleader.

Instead of indulging in any post-mortems, he locked himself at home in his workshop. This was the first time in years that he had had the opportunity of indulging his fondness for mechanics. It had not, he noticed, declined with neglect. He was seized with the spirit of invention as never before and created something which, he felt, could be of use to travelling orchestras. It was publicly displayed when his new band (the sixth) opened in Fort Worth in the summer of 1945. During intermission the thing was carried to the bandstand. The customers eyed it warily. There were excited whispers of, 'What is it?'

'It's a multi-purpose band box,' said Jack. Undismayed by the baffled silence he pressed a button and gave a tug. 'Now it's a table,' he said, 'for gin rummy.' He pulled a lever and out slid a make-up kit complete with mirror. Everybody said it was marvellous except a local journalist who told Jack, 'If you can build a folding bed, barbecue grill, and cold box for brew, you'll really have something.' In his column next day he wrote, 'If America ever needs a secret weapon, Jack Teagarden is the man to build it.' A few days later the cumbersome apparatus was stolen from the club. Its whereabouts still remain a mystery on the records of the Fort Worth police department.

It wasn't the first time Jack's mechanical interest provoked more snickers than serious study. Everyone in the music business knows that he regards any defective apparatus as a challenge to his instincts for repair and is just as strongly tempted to dismantle a perfect unit for no other reason than to rebuild it. Those who know him closely share with him a deeper conviction—that had his inventiveness in jazz not motivated his life, he might have attained distinction in the field of creative engineering.

The new band pursued an unexciting tour of cinemas. It played a week at the Golden Gate Theatre in San Francisco, splitting the bill with *Tarzan of the Amazons*, went on to the Orpheum in Los Angeles as alternate feature to Roy Rogers in *Lights of Old Santa Fe*. Veteran jazz fans still cherished the deathless trombone solos the man had created and forgotten, but very few knew where he was now or what he was doing. That summer, one critic did run across him by chance and wrote of the encounter, 'Teagarden has been a noted man with a horn for some time. It now looks as though he wants to cash in on his experience. He has the name, but his band doesn't live up to it.'

With the end of the war in Europe, transport conditions eased and Chumas acquired a bus for the band. By now Addie was certain that Chumas' hostility towards her concealed something more than jealousy of her interest in the band. More than once she had asked to see the books, but each time she had been brushed off. Finally she told Jack.

'The books are George's business,' he replied curtly.

One evening when Chumas was out of his room, Addie entered, opened the books and was appalled. She called Jack. 'Are these records?' she asked.

He looked at them and shook his head slowly.

'Don't you realize,' she pressed, 'you don't know where you stand financially?'

He sighed and reached for a drink. She was about to tell him it would not do any good but changed her mind, reached for another glass and joined him.

Chumas was fired the following day and Ray Callahan,

Addie's brother-in-law, was called in to take over. Shortly after, a columnist in Sioux Falls wrote, 'Jack Teagarden stepped off a C-47 out on the flight line here looking a little tired but the music he and his band played for a crowd of over 1,000 G.I.s and their dates at the Coliseum in town this week was anything but weary. Since Pearl Harbour he has entertained at more than 500 Army, Navy and Marine Corps Camps throughout the country.'

A nice tribute. But it had cost him national popularity. Now he lost his final band after one more depressing tour. Even the bus disappeared one evening and it was weeks later that he learned Chumas, having purchased it under his own name, had merely reclaimed his 'own' property. Returning to Hollywood, the bandsmen listened, some commiserating, some sullen as Jack told them 'I can't pay you off. You'll have to file your claims with the union'. He paused. Then he added, 'I'm sorry.' After they had gone he reached mechanically for the bottle. When it was empty he reached for another. A girl handed it to him—it wasn't Addie. And this time Louis Armstrong's reassurances were forgotten. Addie walked out of their marriage and into the divorce court.

Jack took a room at the Drake Hotel, shook off a hangover one morning and felt more lonely than he ever had been in his life. He had no band, no wife, no money, no job. He stared dully at his trombone for several minutes and even it seemed alien. A fit of coughing seized him and he shivered. When the coughing continued he called a doctor.

'You've a bronchial condition and severe fatigue,' the doctor told him and ordered him to bed. Long bouts of travel, insufficient rest and hasty meals exacted their toll and his condition had been worsened by the increased tension of recent months.

Before becoming a bandleader he had taken responsibility lightly, convinced that ignoring problems often solved them. As a bandleader he could quite properly entrust administrative tasks to others, leaving himself free to conduct the music.

Too late, he realized it was not that simple. Then he had begun to worry more out of concern for the men who depended upon him than for his own welfare. But worry couldn't set right the appalling accountancy, nor could it repair the damage to his marriage.

In his dark little room at the Drake he tried to worry about Addie. Just then a bellhop brought him an angry reminder from Billie's lawyer that he was behind in his alimony. Others followed, threatening court action. He gave up worrying and tried something else. But liquor didn't help either.

It was December 1946, the beginning of the bleakest winter he had ever known. He got a job in the Susie Q against doctor's orders, fronting a small group which included Charles. He stepped off the stand after the first set to be met by a union official. 'You're seventeen hundred dollars in the red for band wages,' he was told.

'I know. I told the boys to file their claims.'

He went back on the stand and if the half-jaded handful in the club had bothered to listen at all, they might have heard a new despair in the trombonist's playing. For the union man had told him to pay up or his card would be seized.

As for the payment owing his ex-wife, there came a pause in the flow of demands for settlement. 'Maybe she's asking Saint Teresa to work on me,' he told himself. But Billie had been invoking more earthly authority. She had an injunction issued for the seizure of Jack's band library and equipment. It was stored in the Long Beach home and in due time the county sheriff drove out to pick it up.

Addie restrained him. She tried to explain that much of Jack's musical literature consisted of expression, composition and arrangements highly individual in nature which only he could properly interpret. Her arguments failed to impress the sheriff but the bulk of the material he was to appropriate did. He studied the large trunks, said briefly, 'Too heavy,' and drove away.

Addie, genuinely dismayed by Jack's financial dilemma,

offered help. It was not only pride which made him refuse, but a bitterness which distorted his reason, causing him to associate her with the failure of the last band.

It would have been quite easy, in fact, to lay the blame for all his troubles upon wives, careless managers, and plain bad luck. Somewhat to Jack's own astonishment, he refused to do this and admitted to himself that in the last analysis, assuming he ever got past the first, he might find that there was only one person he could honestly hold to account—himself.

The admission brought a sense of relief and enabled him to sing and play at the Susie Q with much more feeling than if he had been utterly crushed by his woes. He sang the blues of every man who was ever disenchanted by life and women and smiled at the few who bothered to listen. He wondered how the smile could come so easily. It wasn't artificial, neither was it of hopeless resignation, although the harsh truth that he was deeply in trouble plainly confronted him. Disregard, his characteristic shield against perplexity, proved effective no longer. Indeed, the problems had destroyed the defences by feeding on them. Grown bigger, they pressed in upon him.

Not until the day after he was forced to quit the Susie Q did he realize how big they really were. He was called to the union office and addressed by a grave-faced official. 'You are heavily in debt.'

'The boys' salaries.' Jack nodded. 'So I've heard.'

'There's more. The band taxes haven't been paid.'

Jack gripped the sides of his chair. 'What can I do? I've nothing left but my horn. Shall I sell it?' His voice rose and trembled. 'Is that what you want?'

The official sighed. 'I'm sorry, Mr. Teagarden. But the amount must be settled.'

'How much is owing?'

'Fourteen thousand dollars.'

The shock purged his mind of any lingering unconcern and left him with a firmer resolve. Here was a challenge only *he* could meet. The pride which had prevented him from accepting Addie's offer of aid refused to let him acquaint his family with the scope of his difficulties. He knew anyway that his mother's income from the piano lessons barely met her own needs. As for Charles, he was himself scuffling for security.

Music, never a stable field, had been made more hazardous by changing popular tastes, wartime economies and revolutionary trends. There was small likelihood, Jack told himself, that he could ever reclaim the position of prominence he had once held. But he could try. He had to.

But not in California. Memories of professional frustration were abundant here, while the house at Long Beach, which Addie had sold after the divorce, stood as a monument to their vanished love. A fresh start would demand total concentration, effort and enthusiasm. He could muster none of these in California.

One evening he went back to the Drake after an idle walk along Vine and found a message awaiting him. It was from Bing Crosby. In response to it he called next day at Bing's office. Crosby studied him for a moment. 'I hear you've got troubles,' he said.

'Bad news travels fast,' Jack said, and recited his catalogue of misfortunes. 'But I'm going to start all over again.'

'You don't have to,' said Crosby. 'Just take up where you left off.'

'Not here. Not in California.'

The singer filled his pipe. 'New York, maybe?'

Jack shrugged.

Crosby buzzed a secretary. 'Make out a cheque to Jack Teagarden for six hundred dollars.' He turned to Jack. 'That should cover your fare and leave some for snacks.'

On his way out, Jack paused. 'It won't be for long, Bing. I'll . . .'

'I know, you'll pay me back.' Bing Crosby grinned. 'Make sure you do. I need the dough, son!'

Chapter IX

IT was the spring of 1947. As he had done twenty years before, Jack arrived in New York unheralded, to begin anew. Much had changed, including the music scene. Something called bop, spawned in Harlem, had spread to 52nd Street and radiated from there. Tagged by journalistic tastemakers as 'dixielanders', jazz musicians unable or unwilling to adopt the new form retreated to the downtown bridgeheads of Nick Rongetti's, Eddie Condon's, and Stuyvesant Casino. The subsequent conflict was waged less by the musicians themselves than by groups of partisans employing bitter words as weapons. Not many years later, members of the rival factions unashamedly fraternized, some even becoming business associates in the field of the very music they had helped tear asunder.

But then, presumably, they regretted splitting jazz into mutually antipathetic schools. They readily forgave each other and themselves the absurdities of the mid-'forties when they substituted for cautious tolerance a derision of all innovation; or for respectful assessment, a flouting of the *status quo*. But the damage their unnecessary war did to jazz and to more than a few talented musicians (especially those who would not be encumbered with the arbitrary labels of 'bop' or 'dixieland'), is impossible to estimate.

By their utter supremacy in the art of jazz, a small number of its exponents defy attempts to classify them with catchwords, cannot be comfortably lodged in any tastemaker's niche, and receive the admiration of all other jazzmen, whatever their styles. Armstrong, Earl Hines, Coleman Hawkins, are examples. So is Jack Teagarden. But when he stepped off the plane at La Guardia that bleak March morning, he was still in a state of professional eclipse. He was not then aware of the acrimonious phase jazz was entering. Nothing, in fact, weighed upon his mind except an urge to work and the immediate need for a cup of coffee. He gave his cap a tug, firmly grasped his trombone case and overnight bag, and strode to the terminal whistling *Sometimes I Feel Like a Motherless Child*. In no way did the song reflect his mood.

After coffee he went straight to the union office. 'Just to let you know I'm here to work,' he reported.

'You can't work,' he was told at once. 'A ruling forbids you to work until your debts are paid off.'

Earlier this fresh blow might have prostrated him. Now he fought back with an urgent appeal for consideration. How could he possibly clear his slate without earning the money to do so? It was an effective argument which won him a hollow victory. He would be allowed to work on condition that a hundred dollars a week be paid towards dissolution of the debt. 'Fine,' said Jack. 'A hundred to the union, fifty to an ex, and how do I eat?' He remembered Jimmy McPartland. 'What's the grasshopper situation around here?'

The union man looked puzzled. 'Never mind,' said Jack and made for the door.

'Tell me, Mr. Teagarden,' the official called after him. 'How did you get into this mess?'

Jack hesitated. 'It was easy,' he said quietly.

He started humbly with a guest appearance over a New York radio station. Someone in the studio remarked that the old Teagarden horn had lost its bite. Had the recent distress enfeebled his playing so that he could never recover? He fought off the fear but had no doubt that his delivery lacked the strength of former days. It would come back. It had to. But it would take time.

After the broadcast he received a call from Ray Callahan, now living in Boston. 'I heard the show,' said Callahan. 'You've sounded better. Anything I can do?'

'You can come down here and manage me.'

Callahan found him in Nick Rongetti's blowing alongside Muggsy Spanier, Ernie Carceres and Miff Mole, veteran musicians whose reliable talents had not been atrophied by the post-war job scarcity. Gradually Jack felt the old confidence creep back. More broadcasts and guest shows followed. Word filtered through jazz circles that Jack Teagarden was not only back in town but he was back on form, willing and able, blowing his accumulated miseries out and away through the bell of his horn. Money flowed again and although it kept flowing right past him on its way to the union and Billie, he withheld enough for beer and steaks at Nick's. He also bought some steam-engine gear which, he found, cushioned the fits of loneliness that often beset him in his hotel room and which a bottle or a babe, any babe, might once have satisfied. These, he was surprised to find, no longer sufficed.

The most eloquent proof of his recovery of prestige was displayed at one of the midnight Town Hall concerts promoted that spring by Ernie Anderson. Although dominated by the incomparable Louis Armstrong, they featured stars of similar magnitude, including the ace drummer Sidney Catlett, Dick Carey, who played the piano and the trumpet with equal skill, and the cornettist Bobby Hackett. Jack heard their names with delight. 'And working with Louis again,' he said to Callahan. 'What more could a guy want?'

But it wasn't all he wanted.

By sheer talent and a quiet determination not always discernible behind his easy-going façade, he had climbed out of despair and back into popular demand. Not as a bandleader (*that* venture was little more than a sometimes nightmarish memory now) but as a single jazz attraction. Still, an irksome need was ever present and, which was more annoying, he knew where the cure might be found, but pride kept him from taking the first step. Then one night he said to Callahan, 'No more rented tuxedos for me. I've got damn' good clothes on the coast.'

'Why don't you call for them?' suggested Callahan.

'They're with Addie.'

'Makes no difference. Call her.'

'Think I will.' Jack crossed to the telephone and paused. He had never lost his distaste for the thing. Suddenly he seized it with such force that Callahan sat up. 'You want to pay for a busted hotel phone?' he said.

Jack didn't answer. He put a call through to California, reached Addie and began a polite and unnecessarily long conversation on the subject of clothes and the impossibility of renting a good tuxedo around Manhattan. Callahan left the room.

When he returned, Jack was still talking. 'We'll get undivorced,' he was saying. He paused. 'Okay, talk to your lawyer.'

'For a guy who hates phones . . .' Callahan began.

Jack hung up. 'Addie's sending my clothes by railway express,' he announced casually.

'Is that all you talked about?'

Jack grinned and poured himself a drink.

On the other side of the country Addie was doing the same. Unsettling though that call had been, she couldn't deny a certain joy in her discomposure. She rallied and telephoned her lawyer. 'What do I do to get married?' she asked.

'Are you serious? You only have an interlocutory decree. You can't marry until it becomes final next March. Who is he?'

'Jack. Jack Teagarden.'

The sounds at the other end of the phone indicated it was the lawyer's turn to take a drink. Impatiently Addie said, 'Well, what do I do?'

'Live together. You're already married.' The lawyer chuckled. 'I'll notify the court. And, Addie?'

'I'm listening.'

'God bless you both.'

Jack received the news while he prepared for the Town Hall concert. In a happier frame of mind than he could remember, he went onstage with Armstrong and Hackett, Peanuts Hucko and Catlett and Dick Carey where they created in solo and ensemble, jazz after their fashion. Everyone was in good humour. Louis Armstrong had just recovered his beloved trumpet after its theft. 'It's like having my woman back,' he exulted. 'Can't get used to another one.'

'I know what you mean,' said Jack and joined him in a rare and rollicking duet on *Rockin' Chair*. Then Louis signalled *Pennies from Heaven* and after his huskily tender vocal Jack entered with a charming trombone passage. During *St. James Infirmary* a hush settled upon the Town Hall audience as he held the water glass to the instrument and conjured the familiar but ever haunting sonorities; after which he sang of past crises with women:

> I was born at midnight, by morning I could talk.
> They called me Casanova, had eyes just like a hawk.'

An ecstasy was abroad that night. It came from the music and was reflected back from the audience to re-inspire the performers. Its effect was sometimes bemusing. Pianist Art Hodes, selected to deliver a eulogy of compere Fred Robbins, lost himself in it and quite forgot Robbins' name. To no one in particular Jack exclaimed, 'I've waited twenty years for this, I'm in heaven tonight.' In his enthusiasm he raised the trombone and began a chorus just as the final curtain fell.

After the concert Anderson shared a taxi to the Apollo Theatre with Louis and Jack. Louis was working there with his band, Jack as a single.

'Why don't you two talk to Joe Glaser about an All Star unit? You're great together.'

Louis looked at Jack and grinned. 'Turn this cab around,' he said to the driver. 'We got business to talk.'

From this chance remark evolved what might have been the most exciting unit in jazz history, but instead proved to be the most perplexing—the Louis Armstrong All Stars.

Chapter X

JACK showed no hesitation in joining the new unit. For one thing, the Glaser venture promised a term of employment which would speedily whittle down the tower of debt still over-shadowing him; and he was uplifted by the prospect of working regularly alongside the jazz musician he most respected. He had shared with Louis Armstrong only a handful of recordings made on just two dates since the memorable *Knockin' a Jug*.

It was August 1947 when the All Stars made their début at Billy Berg's in Hollywood. Although the whole country had been the arena in which each of Jack's big band jousts had suffered defeat, he still considered California his special corner of failure. But as he headed west again his trepidation was banished by an optimistic self-assurance springing from the knowledge that at least for the foreseeable future he would be working in good company. And there was Addie. He had already forgotten the long-distance plea for his clothes which had ended in reaffirmations of mutual need; but the comforting thrill it had aroused stayed with him.

Typically, he failed to telephone but took a cab to her North Hollywood home. After the initial shyness had been banished by an emergency consignment from the near-by liquor store, fresh vows were exchanged and there began a series of days markedly reminiscent of St. Louis in 1941 but without the Piper Cub. The marriage was resumed in such an atmosphere of confident cordiality that its permanence seemed at last assured. But no. With total disregard for anti-climax, Jack and Addie separated again, one year and many tours later.

The entire affair resembled a harmonious concert with smouldering intermissions. But the 1948 rupture was the last; both were beginning to find that reunions, however sweet, could become tediously repetitive. As if conceding that they and fate and the passing years had sufficiently tested their love and left no question of its truth and durability, Jack and Addie returned to each other in a more mature spirit of dedication. Since then, theirs has been a reasonably tranquil union blessed by the arrival of a son.

Throughout the All Stars' years, what of Jack's music? As the unit was born during a mounting interest in newer jazz forms and a corresponding contempt for what was usually (and often incorrectly) dismissed as 'Dixieland', its formation did not stir the jazz world to the extent it should have. After all, this was a band which, with the exception of its young bass player, repre-sented the whole first generation of jazz and contained some of the music's major talent. Armstrong, although not yet a figure of national renown, had long been established as the most gifted liv-ing jazz creator and a powerful link with its founding days. Barney Bigard had long been associated with Duke Ellington but his tone had lost none of the now pensive, now sensuous quality which is a hallmark of so many New Orleans clarinettists. Earl Hines' contribution to jazz is that of a major revolutionary who vastly broadened the scope of the piano as a jazz voice, as Tea-garden and Harrison had done with the trombone. Both Sidney Catlett and his replacement, Cozy Cole, were masters in the use of the drums as a propulsive force rather than mere rhythmic support. Finally, Jack himself had decisively shown a striking authority of jazz utterance, opportunities for which had occurred all too rarely and obviously required the company of his pro-fessional equals. A supreme parity would be established of such measure that it could not help but produce lasting and exciting music.

In view of such wonderful promise the uneven results seem

all the more disappointing. A reason for this, perhaps the most vital, was the change that two decades had wrought on these men, their music, and their attitudes to the music. Since their brief, glorious 'Harlem' period, Hines, Armstrong, Jack had all led big bands at one time or another and experienced the vicissitudes such enterprises involve. Each had tasted the heady flavour of commercial success, each had suffered his share of frustrations. To Armstrong and Hines in particular the frustrations were compounded by their deep conviction that they were outstanding creative musicians whose greatness, by all reports, enjoyed recognition abroad (subsequent foreign tours would confirm this) while at home it went largely unnoticed.

The All Stars visited Washington, D.C., one night in 1950 and played in a huge and ugly sports arena afflicted with miserable acoustics. A large and youthful crowd shuffled uninspiringly around the floor, the sound of its feet competing upsettingly with the echoes from Cozy Cole's drum tattoo.

If the performances of Armstrong, Hines and Jack had any value that night, they could not be heard. The choruses escaped to be lost somewhere amid smoke, shadows and the shredded flags drooping from the roof.

A blond boy left his partner's side, approached the bandstand, beckoned Louis and requested *When the Saints Go Marching In*. He waved a dollar bill. Armstrong studied him for a moment then turned away. He gave a wry grin at Jack. They played *Saints*. At intermission the crowd swarmed to the hot-dog and coke stand. The musicians, left alone, smoked and sat on the hard wooden benches. Louis sat a little apart from the others in an attitude of dejection which contrasted movingly with the ebullience to which he is normally given. If he was silently asking himself whether it was all worth it, nobody could blame him.

Just five years later in the same city, the State Department was publicly lauding the trumpeter for his inestimable worth in winning foreign friends for the U.S.A., and Americans who had all but ignored him as a unique creative artist raved over

Ambassador Satch as the mugging, trumpet-blowing, 'clown' of television and the concert stage.

The irony of this doesn't bother Armstrong today. But it is not unlikely that the earlier apathy shown his serious work planted a cynicism in his character. Less conjectural in the matter of the All Stars is the effect upon their output of playing together, night after night, to the same type of chattering customers; following the same deadening programme, making the same humourless gags about singer Velma Middleton's girth and Bigard's baldness; blowing the same tired clichés behind Miss Middleton's disquieting and regularly tasteless endeavours; marching round a cramped stage to *Saints*, a sheepish routine which recalled to Jack the embarrassing Pollack-Foyer inventions. Responsibility for what appeared to be dogged adherence to insipidity rests at least in part upon Armstrong himself. In extenuation, the public applauded it as drollery and the band's bookers were undoubtedly convinced that if he didn't serve it, Armstrong would cease to be a profitable attraction.

Time had introduced an abundance of conceits into Earl Hines' piano playing although his technical brilliance was undiminished. Earl's flashiness and Armstrong's showmanship sometimes clashed to spark personal friction. On these occasions Jack maintained a tight-lipped neutrality. The close Hines-Armstrong partnership of the late 'twenties, the incomparable duo of *Weather Bird, Two Deuces, West End Blues*, and *Skip the Gutter* was a thing of the past. Similarly, the Armstrong-Teagarden affinity spontaneously achieved during *Knockin' a Jug* and lamentably deprived of the opportunity of development, was another brief glory impossible to revive. No conscious effort was put forward to recover them. Most musicians, when challenged by a nostalgic minority to resume earlier styles, reply with justification that you cannot live in the past, you cannot stand still; in the jazz game you must keep moving. It is unfair and absurd to expect a jazz musician to play the same way all his life.

The debate often fails to consider an important truth about

the history of jazz so far. It is that even if a jazz man earnestly wishes always to blow in the manner instinctive to him, even if he is profoundly sure he is 'playing the truth', the music's still groping youth, its sudden and wayward trends, its relation to society, its professional dilemmas, its involvement with race prejudice, its commercial exactions, some part or all of this unique texture encompassing the American jazz musician will affect or wholly alter his method of expression at some stage of his career. He *must* change whether he wants to or not.

The All Stars chapter was not one of entirely unfulfilled promise. Commercially, it was a highly successful venture and materially benefited all hands.

Jack was enabled to dissolve his debts and plan a bright future for Addie and their son. Whenever he could do so, he also pursued his cherished hobby to the frequent mystification of Louis and Earl. Once, explaining magnetism to Armstrong and clearly not making much progress, Jack illustrated with the aid of flashlight batteries, wires and nails. At the end of the experiment Louis shook his head in awe. 'Jack, I still don't know about this magnetism,' he said gruffly, 'but I'll bet you could invent an atom bomb, put your mind to it.'

Inevitably there were unpleasant interludes when the band entered the South. But unexpectedly encouraging ones as well. Armstrong avoided Memphis altogether because the authorities would not allow a mixed group on the stage. But in Houston, where the audience was separated into white and coloured sections, the music soon exerted a spell which had the fans flocking to the stage in one joyful unsegregated mass. 'And,' chuckled Louis, recalling the incident, 'nobody is looking around to see who's behind them.'

When the band played at Negro beach resorts along the Carolina coast, the restrictions of 'white territory' were forgotten, the music and merriment less restrained. Thoughtful elements among the audiences would seek Jack's company and with careful nonchalance try to remove any sense of solitariness. Their kind efforts were unnecessary for he had none. He felt wholly at ease, stayed out of the more strenuous conviviality,

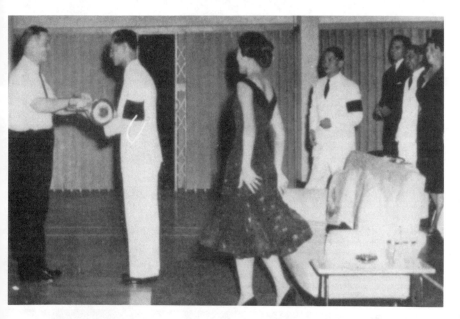

The King of Siam is presented with a trombone by Jack, and
(*below*) they followed up with a jam session, the King playing
on alto saxophone

At the end of his exhausting tour, and still racked by illness, Jack Teagarden in a Tokyo TV studio sat back, stretched his legs and in his own words 'watched all the people enjoy themselves'.

There were heartbreaks too. Overnight in Albuquerque, Jack was unable to endure the sight of his colleagues being forced by discrimination into a sleazy, rat-infested hotel. Angrily, he hailed a cab and prowled the town until he found more civilized accommodation for them.

These and other harrassments, not to mention backstage dissension, could not prevent the creation of much fine music. Dissatisfied though the diehard minority might be with their output of good jazz, it was impossible for the All Stars to play bad jazz. The records which this unit made, like its nightclub and concert appearances, contain much stirring music to offset the stretches of hollow showmanship, the vexing patches of dullness when lassitude weakened the strands of unity.

Its two European tours brought to that continent the best display of live jazz it had ever known, gave multitudes the opportunity to meet in person the fabulous figures they had admired from a distance, and boosted an already widespread interest in American jazz to phenomenal dimensions. The moments of grand jazz which irregularly illumine its career occurred often enough to justify judgment of the All Stars band as a project of substantial worth which, although possessing all the essentials, failed to make history. Its dissolution was inevitable. Jack, after five years of unvarying routine, felt that he had exhausted his capacity for adding anything new. Hines had long before made it clear that when Jack left, he would follow. From loyalty to both Armstrong and Glaser, Jack had already extended his tenure several times, but it was Addie's pregnancy which finally solved his dilemma.

Chapter XI

AFTER his severance from the All Stars, Jack worked locally and intermittently, spending as much time as he could at home with his son. Never had he so fully realized the pleasures of parenthood, the adventures it could bring. Leisurely rambles through Griffith Park alternated with fast motor-scooter jaunts along the roads lacing Hollywood Hills. Jack would be at the wheel, Joey riding backseat and clutching his father with scared delight. It was a carefree existence.

The Suzie Q, scene of past frustrations, was content to have Jack working there again, and he was even more pleased as the club was only a five-minute drive from home. As the entire Teagarden clan now clustered around Hollywood, Jack, Charles and Norma formed the nucleus of a satisfying small band which also included Ray Bauduc (drums), Kas Malone (bass) and Jay St. John, a clarinet-playing ex-postman. Inevitably, travelling began. After a few months on the road the unit split; Norma grew concerned about her mother, and Charles, preferring to stay near his family, returned to a steady daytime job with Bob Crosby's TV show.

An uneventful period followed until Capitol Records, with whom Jack contracted in 1955, issued the first of several albums containing proof that desultory employment had not atrophied Jack's high talents. In 1956, under an Anglo-U.S. jazz exchange programme launched after a twenty years' ban on foreign musicians performing in Britain, Jack was invited to form a band for a British tour.

His visit to continental Europe while a member of the Armstrong All Stars was the closest he had been to his British fans, but such was their devotion (in many cases dating back to Ben Pollack days) that when they saw him in person for the first time it was as a meeting of old friends. His arrival on English soil had other aspects, too. It had been hoped by adult British jazz-lovers that visits from some of the best American players would not only stimulate local musicians but might also convince the nation's youth that there were more edifying forms of American music than rock 'n' roll, that this noisy aberration was nothing but a distant and disreputable cousin of jazz, best shunned in favour of the authentic article.

Those who felt this way looked to the visitors for support. To their despair, not all the Americans seemed to know or care about the responsibility this implied. Of course, the devotees had heard all about the seamier environment of their favourite music and knew that jazz musicians are somewhat lower than the angels. Nevertheless, they experienced a shock when, for example, a notable figure whose visit had been eagerly antici-pated by thousands who had admired him from afar, staggered from his plane at London Airport in a state of drunken collapse. During the subsequent tour, public inebriation and a drooling contempt for his audiences drew cries of 'Go home and sober up'. Until he heeded this and kindred advice from concert promoters and his colleagues, the tour, if not the whole ex-change programme, seemed threatened with fiasco.

The bad taste left by this episode had not entirely vanished when Jack, Max Kaminsky (trumpet), Peanuts Hucko (clarinet), Jack Lesberg (bass), Earl Hines (piano) and Cozy Cole (drums) reached England. In the meantime, Count Basie's Orchestra had stormed the country, earning popular praise and royal attention. But Basie's formidably disciplined unit was in a separate class. Small, less formal jazz bands were still suspect.

Matters were further clouded by the melancholy events in Little Rock, which reached a climax on the very eve of Jack's

arrival. Outside their own country, jazz musicians often appear
to be regarded as oracles of opinion on U.S. domestic affairs.
In America, on the other hand, it occurs to few that jazz musicians might have any political viewpoints worth airing. When
Louis Armstrong declaimed on Little Rock and the American
President, it was this fact as much as the vehemence of his
oratory which made Americans everywhere sit up and take
notice.

Jack's statement to the London Press was less sensational.
'We play unsegregated music,' he said. 'And our band is unsegregated. Race doesn't bother us one bit. Little Rock?' He
grinned. 'I'll try and get Earl here to play *Little Rock Getaway.*
That will take care of Little Rock.' Which remark was neither
provocative nor enlightening. The reporters drifted away, dis-
armed and baffled.

After a successful opening in Royal Festival Hall, Jack's
provincial concerts began by breaking attendance records at St.
Andrew's Hall, Glasgow, where two hundred excited Scotsmen
left their seats at the end of the show and mobbed the musicians
in their dressing-rooms. The tour continued as a series of
triumphs despite an Asian 'flu epidemic which dogged it. As
none of the band displayed any excessive thirst, camp followers
who kept trying to force whisky on them were confounded; and
the stigma of insobriety which had shadowed every American
jazzman coming to Britain was largely removed.

But newspaper reports contained a few mildly startling im-
pressions. According to the *Daily Mail,* Jack's 'morocco-
skinned face looked like a burst football when he grinned' and
'his silk-lazy horn and grated-cheese voice', etc. The *Daily
Express* described him as 'sleek', an adjective better applied
surely to Earl Hines who 'alternately wisecracked and pounced
at the keyboard like a playful black panther'. Still, the attention
they received from Britain's popular Press was wholly favourable
and more lavish than they were accustomed to getting at home.

For their part, the Americans thought highly of Britain's
musicians, some of whom had greeted them at the airport with
a raucously warm welcome. Shortly after his return to the U.S.,

Jack was privately asked if his praise for the Scottish trumpeter, Alex Welsh, wasn't just a polite and natural guise for the gratitude which British hospitality had aroused in him. 'Nothing of the sort,' he replied. 'Welsh is a first-class musician, the equal of any youngster I've heard in the States.'

Critical response to the first Teagarden tour of Britain was fairly uniform. Immaculate as the leader unquestionably was, his restraint on the stage surprised even those who are well aware that whatever else Jack is, he is no showman. His characteristic reserve was emphasized by the cold which plagued him (the Manchester Free Trade Hall concert was delayed half an hour while he was given anti-'flu injections), and above all by the unbridled exhibitionism of Earl Hines.

Almost every concert review stated that Earl Hines stole the show. His astonishing display may well have been a manifestation of resentment over having to share top billing. A surmise not unfair to him, for Hines is one of the most brilliant creators in jazz and nobody knows this better than Hines. Alternately simmering and flashing, he is not easily outshone. When he worked with Armstrong, the latter's strong radiance could equal and sometimes eclipse him. But Jack's modest demeanour, Hucko's mild style, Kaminsky's self-discipline, none of these was any match for Hines' personality. The only challenge to his command of the limelight came from the explosive Cole.

A belief was expressed on all sides that Jack should assume a more aggressive stage manner. However, while unable to underrate Hines' talents, the English critics did not overlook the subdued leader. 'Teagarden was impeccable in everything he did,' Max Jones wrote in the *Melody Maker*. 'His playing, long ago refined of all impurities, looks deceptively easy. And this, taken into conjunction with his apologetic manner, can lull you into thinking that not much is happening.' To which a fellow reviewer added, 'I don't go along with those who say that Tea should "push" himself. I think he's managing wonderfully well just as he is.'

In the closing months of 1958, under an arrangement between the American National Theatre and Academy and the U.S.

State Department, Jack took a jazz unit to the Far East, to parts
of the globe where the music had never been heard before. His
route crossed mountains, jungles and oceans, touched remote
hamlets and rice villages as well as all the major cities. Whether
viewed as an ambitious step towards the ideal of cultural exchange, or as the cold war weapon some Americans have termed
it, the policy of dispatching jazz bands to foreign countries
might prove to have a broadening effect not only upon international friendships but on jazz itself. It is encouraging to note
that most jazzmen selected for these trips, refusing to consider
them solely as long-distance gigs or junkets, have displayed
genuine interest in forms and techniques of foreign music.

Jack's tour of the Orient, the most extensive undertaken in
that area by American musicians, became a mission of discovery
as well as entertainment. He summarized this theme in Tokyo's
Sankei Hall following one of the last concerts of the tour. 'My
experiences these past weeks have convinced me as nothing else
could that everyone in the world has music to give and everyone
something to learn. In all the places I have played, I have been
listening to music, the music of the people who live there.'

And not only listening. He carried a portable tape recorder
everywhere, studied native styles as much as his tight schedule
allowed, and never ceased marvelling at the countless examples he witnessed of the potential in music for creating
friendships between peoples of different language and culture.

The usually turbulent East seemed more so during Jack's
penetration of it. Three countries underwent swift and sudden
(but happily bloodless) changes of régime as the jazzmen
travelled through, and tension in the Formosa Straits had
reached an ominous pitch when they flew across from Hong
Kong to give performances on the hills outside Taipeh. Since
the United States' attitude to each political development did
not have the unanimous approval of Easterners, an apprehension existed among the organizers of the tour that the visiting
Americans might be received in some areas with coolness,
suspicion or open hostility.

It was a tribute to the host countries, the guests and the music they dispensed that nothing marred the strong East-West rapport established at Kabul on September 25th, 1958, and sustained along a 17,000-mile itinerary to Tokyo in January of the following year. At a time when fear and distrust filled the world's headlines, and presumably people's hearts, as rarely before, it is also somewhat comforting.

The quiet pride Jack felt at being chosen was shared by Addie. But as the departure date came near, her attention was wholly dominated by a wave of problems ranging from visas and inoculations to less prosaic matters such as the need for the music of a dozen or more national anthems at short notice. (That of India was obtained from the Minneapolis Symphony Orchestra, but since it was scored for ninety-six instruments and no piano, Jack rescored it for small band. His arrangement is now standard for future jazz groups visiting that country.) But however challenging to her managerial capacities at the outset, the tour was to test Addie's fortitude—and Jack's—in grim fashion before it ended.

Max Kaminsky, whose system had not entirely recovered from its encounter with British hotel fare, wondered what dietary challenges awaited it in the East. As it turned out, the exotic foods he tasted along the way did nothing to impair his prowess on trumpet. Don Ewell, the one member of the band unable to take his instrument, was only mildly anxious about the condition of the pianos there. How could they be any worse than some he had been obliged to work on at home? Ronnie Greb (drums) and Stan Puls (bass) pondered the possibility of severe temperature changes on skins and strings, but uppermost in their thoughts was the exciting try-out promised for their new camera equipment. Clarinettist Jerry Fuller already had a specific photographic objective: the site and remains, if any, of the *Bridge on the River Kwai*, filmed in Ceylon.

Although the U.S. State Department Information Service supplied concert promoters with appropriate data on the touring musicians, local interpretation and amplification produced some odd results. 'Teagarden is not much of a sportsman,' said a feature writer in the Afghanistan organ *Islah*. 'He is fifty-three now and spends most of his time playing with a toy train which he has installed in his apartment. This play is considered to be a sport in many American clubs which boast quite a heavy membership. Teagarden is a frequent visitor to these clubs.'

But the interest of the people in American jazz was enthusiastic and undoubtedly genuine. A professor of political science in Patna, India, gave ten-minute lectures daily for two weeks prior to the band's arrival, by which time the audience had attained an erudition which would not have shamed Marshall Stearns. While in India, Jack invited local percussion artists on to the stage. 'From the cute little tabas you have here,' he told them, 'clear up to the big kettledrum they have in a symphony orchestra, it's the rhythm that counts.'

Shirtsleeved and solemn, he presented the King of Thailand with a trombone, and afterwards invited His Majesty to join in a jam session. The young monarch did so—on an alto saxophone. A number of gifts and awards were bestowed on the visitors. The President of Burma granted them tenderfoot membership in the Rangoon Boy Scouts. King Norodom Suramarit of Cambodia declared Jack Teagarden an officer of the Order of Merit of Monisaraphan, and presented him with three books of Cambodian music which included the King's own compositions. In Hong Kong the Chai Wan Girl's Club gave him a silken banner while three thousand, five hundred youngsters packing the Wah Yan College auditorium clapped and shouted '*Ho Yeh, Ho Yeh*'.

On December 8th the band landed in Singapore and met the Press in the lobby of the Cathay Hotel where Jack—characteristically without intent—precipitated the affair of *Singapore Sorrows*. It is best described in local news reports.

From the *Straits Times** of December 9th: ' "I have not seen Singapore but I kind of know what it is like," said Mr. Teagarden yesterday. "Benny Pollack and I arranged a wonderful tune called *Singapore Sorrows* twenty-five years ago. It was written by a Singapore composer—I forget his name now but

* The authors are grateful to the Editor of the *Straits Times* for his permission to make quotations from the issues indicated.

it struck me that Singapore was just like that—beautiful, melodious and wonderful. I always dreamt of seeing the place to check but a twenty-five-year wait isn't so bad." '

December 10th: 'Old-timers here have dug deep into the musical past in a search for the composers of the Dixieland melody *Singapore Sorrows* which the American jazz trombonist fell in love with more than twenty-five years ago. While none of the old-timers could be exactly sure who was the composer or composers, the consensus was that there were two—Roy Minjoot and Joe Fernandez. Mr. Minjoot's brother Joe set out tonight to contact Mr. Fernandez, sixty, a government pensioner in Pulau Tekong. Mr. Joe Minjoot, fifty-eight, said, "It will be just wonderful if Roy and Joe receive their well-earned reward after all these years. We all played together in Roy's band, The Scamps, in the early nineteen-twenties. When it came to composing Roy used to write the music and Joe the lyrics." Bandleader Gerry Soliano was excited when he heard that Mr. Minjoot could contact Mr. Fernandez. "This is great," he said. "I am myself quite sure that it was Roy and Joe Fernandez. Roy was a great pianist and Joe used to love writing poetry and things like that. Mr. Teagarden has touched a magic chord bringing to life again the fond and nostalgic memories of Western music here. As I remember the tune was sort of mournful. Parts of it had to do with Chinatown and the girls here. But you know it's a long time and everything is now so vague."

'Mr. N. Collins, secretary of the Musicians' Union here, said he met Roy Minjoot in India six years ago. "He was a dashing character," Mr. Collins said. "He had just left the band of the Maharajah of Bikaner and introduced himself to me as Roy Menjou—a relative of Adolph Menjou."

'Last night Mr. Teagarden told the *Straits Times*, "I'll be really happy to meet the composers. I'd like to play the tune again but of course no one can predict if it will become a hit." '

December 11th: 'The composers of *Singapore Sorrows*, a melody which Jack Teagarden fell in love with more than twenty-five years ago, have now been named. But it seems they are not Singaporeans as Mr. Teagarden said he thought they were.

Commander Billings, U.S. Navy attaché here, found a 1926 record of the song after searching through his jazz library. The label on the record names the composers—Jack le Soir and Ray Doll. Commander Billings thinks they were California musicians. Some Singapore old-timers had thought that two local musicians Roy Minjoot and Joe Fernandez had co-operated on the song. Mr. Joe Minjoot, Roy's brother said, "Well, I'm a little disappointed but I suppose it's quite conclusive now who the composers are." Commander Billings said his discovery was "pure luck". '

By then Jack was safely aboard a plane, *en route* to Kuala Lumpur.

The closing weeks of the tour were jeopardized by illness. Most of the band suffered from what might legitimately be called Asian 'flu, caused by the rapid change from the heat of mainland Asia to the winter temperatures of Korea and Japan. In Taipeh City Hall, Formosa, Stan Puls' stomach began to bother him. After an uncomfortable flight across the Pacific to Okinawa where the band played at a couple of concerts, he was rushed to the hospital and found to require an urgent appendicectomy. Without a bass player the band continued north to Japan where, in an unexpected vein of stubbornness, the Tokyo promoters demanded an all-American band and refused to permit a Japanese replacement. The reason for this, it was explained, was that the audiences would not feel that there was a Japanese jazzman worthy of working the bass in Jack's company.

The U.S. Army came to the rescue. Lee Ivory, a Negro clerk and an occasional bass player, was given temporary leave from his duties with the Army newspaper *Stars and Stripes* and loaned to the Teagarden band for the rest of the tour. At first, low level military bureaucracy caused Private Ivory a few moments of discomfort when he found they were carrying him A.W.O.L. on their rolls. It took a combined operation involving Addie and two generals to straighten things out. But nothing could relieve Private Ivory's nervousness at receptions and similar high level functions when it seemed to him that every high-ranking military and diplomatic figure was present. He had to fight the impulse to salute every time he was introduced. Still, plucking the bass for Jack Teagarden was a proud experience, a never-to-be-forgotten memory, and except for moments when his irregular beat betrayed his nervousness, Private Ivory filled the breach.

Sickness struck at the leader himself, reducing the final stage of his tour to a physical ordeal. The symptoms, painful and ugly, had first been noticed in Laos. Addie reported them to a Philippino doctor in the area and since telephone communication was impossible, had to take a harrowing jeep ride through the jungles to find him. A later and more satisfactory liaison with medical authorities in Saigon revealed the truth. Jack was suffering from acute uremia. The doctor at the U.S. Embassy spoke bluntly. 'You should fly to Manila at once for treatment.'

Jack refused. For one thing, he deeply abhorred hospitals. But there was another reason. Without a trace of heroics in his stance, he felt a deep concern for the job he was doing and the men he led. 'Just give me something to kill the pain,' he said. 'My back's killing me.'

'I'm sorry,' the doctor replied. 'I could give you drugs right now but that pain is the only guide to the seriousness of your condition.' He looked at Addie, then at Jack. 'And I don't mind telling you we already know it's bad.'

The state of Jack's health was flashed through diplomatic channels to the State Department and A.N.T.A. The latter's reaction was immediate. 'Bring him home.'

'It's up to you,' Addie told her husband. She knew this was a decision he wanted to make for himself. Even if she worked on him and won, if she got him to break off the tour now, he would never forgive her. In any case, her powers of persuasion were less than irresistible. The events of the past weeks had taken their toll on her stamina.

Fortified by penicillin and vitamins, Jack resumed the tour. Much of the time he forgot his discomfort while working; and the few drugs which Addie was able to obtain controlled the pain except when its intensity broke through to dull his eyes and blanch his face. But he never missed a show. Though forced to curtail his attendance at parties and receptions he was on the stage for every performance. In Tokyo he granted a Japanese trombonist named Tohru Mori the signal honour of blowing alongside the American master. Within a Hiroshima auditorium Jack was less aware of his physical troubles than of a strange and profoundly moving emotion. For here, on the very site of the core of the bomb's blast, Hiroshima's citizens gave the musicians from America their biggest ovation.

As the plane carrying the travel-weary jazzmen home crossed the Californian coast, those cheers still rang in Jack's ears. Neither would he soon forget the delight on the faces of the many thousands of children they had entertained—Burma Boy Scouts, Pakistan students, Hong Kong waifs, Korean war orphans, the children of kings and presidents and the children who would never know their parents. To all of them, for a moment at least, he and his colleagues had brought some joy. That alone made the whole journey worthwhile.

He felt tired and flashes of pain seared his back and sides. Addie was exhausted and noticeably thinner. The boys in the band, loaded with memories and countless feet of colour film, would welcome a few weeks' rest. They had all done a good job, a damned good job. 'We've been sent out here by the President of the United States and the State Department,' he had announced often and proudly to his audiences. He thought back over the months and couldn't recall a time when he or his musicians had misbehaved or said the wrong thing. Perhaps his *Singapore Sorrows* remark, innocent enough, was the only *faux pas* of the tour, he reflected with a smile. One thing he was sure of. If it had been his purpose to take America's music to the people of the Far East, then he and his band had surely *played* the right thing. Yes, he mused, fastening his safety-belt as the plane began losing altitude, it had been a successful trip, especially when you figured the number of friends you made in all those different countries. That ought to make the President and the Secretary of State happy.

The plane came into Los Angeles Airport at 5 a.m. and the band filed out. Jack blinked. 'Home,' he said.

'No place like it,' Addie murmured and looked around.

There wasn't a soul on hand to greet them.

The next day Jack went into the hospital where the doctors not only operated to relieve his current trouble but repaired a troublesome hernia as well. Then, after six weeks of recuperation he slipped back in the old routine of club dates and one-nighters. Ideas and memories filled his mind; the touching hospitality of the Eastern peoples, their strange music which he intended somehow to combine with his own music in a truly international record album; the courteous care and respect shown them by American diplomatic personnel along the way; Jack felt strongly about these things and spoke of them to anyone who showed interest.

But interest is a quality not often found among nightclub audiences. Sometimes he referred to his tour between numbers, and a few heads would lift at near-by tables upon his mention of a State Department assignment. But, as always in nightclubs, the laughter and noisy chatter never stilled, not even when he played the King of Cambodia's tune. Despite the interval of hospitalization, the transition from the heady experience of his foreign conquests to the uninspiring, disinterested and seemingly interminable rut of jazz on the home front was too great. He felt vaguely and unjustly let down.

Coda

JACK TEAGARDEN has never displayed any violent resentment at the occasional injustices which he knows mar today's jazz scene. A weary indifference to them replaced the quiet disgust he used to show, but this has in turn been largely dispelled by the Far East tour of 1958-9. He returned from his travels physically weakened but spiritually refreshed. An idealism had taken hold of him, though he was unsure how best to express it other than in the form of an international record album which would link the music of the East with American jazz.

Despite the anticlimactic, humdrum routine which he resumed on his return, the zeal which gripped him was and is likely to endure. It should not be permitted to founder. An exciting new concept of cultural exchange is opening before mankind as the world enters the nineteen-sixties. With increasing and more rapid global travel plus a much longed-for relaxing of international tensions and acrimonies, the music of every race will become familiar to all. This is a more thrilling prospect than seems to have been hitherto realized. And weighing his professional experience, sincere personality and simple idealism —above all, the prestige he has already established abroad— a role in it must be assigned for Jack Teagarden.

Then he may find greater inspiration for musical accomplishment than is presently available. It must be said that his trombone work sometimes suffers from a reliance on old phrases which, frequently employed, have become clichés. Clearly, after a lifetime spent within an often jading and frustrating profession, some new source of inspiration would be valuable.

Technically, his playing is flawless, the sense of *pitch* as unerring as ever. The deep and rough emotionalism of treasured old records is gone, but its decline, however regrettable, permits an evaluation of Jack as a swinging, popular entertainer. Gimmickry and showmanship he avoids, which accounts for the fact that he will never reach the top twenty or whatever the current disc jockey scoreboard happens to be. But, as Hoagy Carmichael once shrewdly remarked, 'Teagarden is one of the best things that ever appeared on the popular music scene.'

But it is in jazz where his supreme achievements lie. He is a master of restraint and taste, and if his horn and voice lack the urgency of an earlier day, beneath everything that he plays and sings runs an undercurrent of emotion, a built-in quality of sadness relieved by a hint, barely perceptible, of gentle banter. Where other jazz musicians progress from point zero through a plurality of choruses to a shattering explosion of feeling, the temperature of Teagarden's mood is set from the very first note and sustained with deceptive ease.

In his profession few men are more beloved. He cannot mug, clown or cavort on stage and after forty years in the music business he still registers shyness. Asked not long ago for his own theory of why he plays the way he does, he replied, 'I have none. How can I? All that I've played, all that I've sung, I couldn't have done any other way.' He shook his head at the interviewer. 'I'm nothing super, that's a cinch.'

The unsorted tributes crowding his home in the Hollywood Hills say otherwise. Taken at random, one comes from a citizen of Stockholm and sums up simply all the others. 'Thanks to you, thanks to you for lovely music.'

Selected Discography

THE following is a selected listing of records upon which Jack Teagarden is featured, giving the main soloists. All are either long play or extended play items. When a record has been deleted from the catalogue it is marked with an asterisk. Such records may still be bought from specialist jazz record dealers in some instances. Only American and British issue numbers are listed; the latter can be recognized by the fact that immediately after the name of the label the sign (E) is given. All record labels are given in full, but abbreviations used are:

alt	=alto saxophone	*d*	=drums
arr	=arranger	*g*	=guitar
bar	=baritone saxophone	*p*	=piano
bj	=banjo	*tbn*	=trombone
bs	=string bass	*ten*	=tenor saxophone
clt	=clarinet	*tpt*	=trumpet
c-mel	=c melody saxophone	*vcl*	=vocalist
cnt	=cornet	*vln*	=violin

October 15th, 1928
BEN POLLACK AND HIS CENTRAL
  PARK ORCHESTRA
Jimmy McPartland (*cnt*); Jack
  Teagarden (*tbn*); Benny
  Goodman (*clt*).
Buy, Buy, for Baby   Label X LX3003*
Bashful Baby

January 28th, 1929
BEN'S BAD BOYS
Ben Pollack group featuring
  Jimmy McPartland (*cnt*);
  Jack Teagarden (*tbn*).
Shirt Tail Stomp   Camden CAL-446

February 8th, 1929
EDDIE CONDON'S HOT SHOTS
Leonard Davis (*tpt*); Jack Tea-
  garden (*tbn, vcl*); Happy
  Cauldwell (*ten*); Mezz Mezz-
  row (*c-mel*).
That's a Serious Thing   Label X LX3005*, Camden
                                           CAL-383, Camden (E)
                                           CDN112

*I'm Gonna Stomp Mr. Henry
  Lee* (Takes 1 and 2)   Label X LX3005*

February 1929
THE WHOOPEE MAKERS
Jimmy McPartland (*cnt*); Jack
  Teagarden (*tbn, vcl*).
Makin' Friends   Folkways FP67

March 5th, 1929
LOUIS ARMSTRONG AND HIS
  ORCHESTRA
Louis Armstrong (*tpt*); Jack
  Teagarden (*tbn*); Happy
  Cauldwell (*ten*); Joe Sulli-
  van (*p*).
Knockin' a Jug   Columbia ML54386,
                                           Philips (E) BBL7218

June 11th, 1929
LOUISIANA RHYTHM KINGS
Red   Nichols   (*tpt*);   Jack

Teagarden *(tbn)*; Pee Wee
Russell *(clt)*.

Basin Street Blues   Folkways FP67

September 25th, 1929
MOUND CITY BLUE BLOWERS
Jack Teagarden *(tbn)*; Eddie
Condon *(bj)*; Red McKenzie
(vcl).

Tailspin Blues   Label X LX3005*, HMV
Never Had a Reason to Believe   (E) 7EG80/96*
in You

February 19th, 1931
CHARLESTON CHASERS
Charlie Teagarden *(tpt)*; Jack
Teagarden *(tbn, vcl)*; Glenn
Miller *(tbn, arr)*; Larry Bin-
yon *(ten)*; Benny Goodman
(clt); Gene Krupa *(d)*.

Basin Street Blues   Columbia CL821
Beale Street Blues

October 22nd, 1931
EDDIE LANG-JOE VENUTI AND
   THEIR ALL STAR ORCHESTRA
   Charlie Teagarden *(tpt)*; Jack
   Teagarden *(tbn, vcl)*; Benny
   Goodman *(clt)*; Joe Venuti
   (vln); Eddie Lang *(g)*.

Beale Street Blues   Folkways FP67

November 11th, 1933
JACK TEAGARDEN WITH
   ORCHESTRAL ACCOMPANIMENT
Frank Guarante *(tpt)*; Jack Tea-
   garden *(tbn, vcl)*; Jimmy
   Dorsey *(clt, alt)*.

Love Me	Jolly Roger 5026*
Blue River	
A Hundred Years from Today	—
I Just Couldn't Take it Baby	—

October 18th, 1933
BENNY GOODMAN AND HIS
 ORCHESTRA
Charlie Teagarden (*tpt*); Jack
 Teagarden (*tbn, vcl*); Benny
 Goodman (*clt*); Joe Sullivan
 (*p*); Gene Krupa (*d*).

I Gotta Right to Sing the Blues	Columbia B-1806, Colum-
	bia (E) SEG7806
Aint'cha Glad	— —
Dr. Heckle and Mr. Jibe	— —
Texas Tea Party	— —

November 27th, 1933
BENNY GOODMAN AND HIS
 ORCHESTRA
Shirley Clay, Charlie Teagarden (*tpt*); Jack Teagarden
 (*tbn, vcl*); Benny Goodman
 (*clt*); Joe Sullivan (*p*); Dick
 McDonough (*g*); Gene Krupa
 (*d*); Billie Holiday (*vcl*).

Your Mother's Son-in-Law	Columbia CL821

December 12th, 1933

Keep on Doin' What You're Doin'	—
Riffin' the Scotch	—
Love Me or Leave Me	—
Why Couldn't it be Poor Little Me	—

March 2nd, 1934
JACK TEAGARDEN WITH
 ORCHESTRAL ACCOMPANIMENT
Charlie Teagarden (*tpt*); Jack
 Teagarden (*tbn, vcl*); Jimmy

Dorsey (*clt*); Hilton Lamare
(*g, vcl*).

| *Fare Thee Well to Harlem* | Jolly Roger 5026* |
| *Ol' Pappy* | — |

May 14th, 1934
BENNY GOODMAN AND HIS
ORCHESTRA
Charlie Teagarden (*tpt*); Jack
Teagarden (*tbn, vcl*); Benny
Goodman (*clt*); Teddy Wil-
son (*p*).

Moonglow	Columbia CL821
I Ain't Lazy, I'm Just Dreamin'	Jolly Roger 5023*
As Long as I Live	—

September 18th, 1934
JACK TEAGARDEN WITH
ORCHESTRAL ACCOMPANIMENT
Charlie Teagarden (*tpt*); Jack
Teagarden (*tbn, vcl*); Benny
Goodman (*clt*); Frankie
Trumbauer (*alt*); Casper
Reardon (*harp*).

Stars Fell on Alabama	Jolly Roger 5026*
Your Guess is Just as Good as	
Mine	Folkways FP67
Junk Man	—

April 30th, 1938
JACK TEAGARDEN AND HIS
SWINGIN' GATES
Bobby Hackett (*cnt*); Jack Tea-
garden (*tbn, vcl*); Pee Wee
Russell (*clt*); Bud Freeman
(*ten*); Jess Stacy (*p*).

Meet Me Tonight in Dreamland	Commodore FL20015
Diane	––
Serenade to a Shylock	—

January 12th, 1939
ALL STAR BAND
Bunny Berigan, Harry James
    (*tpt*);   Jack   Teagarden,
    Tommy Dorsey (*tbn*); Benny
    Goodman (*clt*); Eddie Miller
    (*ten*); Bob Zurke (*p*).
Blue Lou   Camden CAL-426, Camden
The Blues   (E) CDN-122

February 7th, 1940
METRONOME ALL STAR BAND
Harry James, Ziggy Elman
    (*tpt*); Jack Teagarden (*tbn*);
    Benny Goodman (*clt*); Benny
    Carter (*alt*); Eddie Miller
    (*ten*); Jess Stacy (*p*); Charlie
    Christian (*g*).
King Porter Stomp   Harmony HL7044
All Star Strut   —

July 23rd, 1940
BUD FREEMAN AND HIS FAMOUS
    CHICAGOANS
Max Kaminsky (*tpt*); Jack Tea-
    garden (*tbn*, *vcl*); Bud Free-
    man (*ten*); Pee Wee Russell
    (*clt*); Dave Tough (*d*).
Jack Hits the Road   Harmony HL7046, Colum-
                                        bia (E) 33S1/016*

47th and State   —   —
Muskrat Ramble   —   —
That Da Da Strain   —   —
Shimme-Sha-Wabble   —   —
At the Jazz Band Ball   —   —
After Awhile   —   —
Prince of Wails   —   —

1940-4
BIG TEA PLAYS THE BLUES
Miscellaneous big band sides led
  by Jack Teagarden (*tbn, vcl*)
  with uncertain personnel.

The Blues	Ultraphonic 1656
Aunt Hagar's Blues	—
Royal Garden Blues	—
Basin Street Blues	—
Shine	—
King Porter Stomp	—
Boogie Woogie	—
Mighty Lak' a Rose	—
Chinatown, My Chinatown	—
East of the Sun	—
China Boy	—
Hindustan	—

December 1944
JACK TEAGARDEN AND HIS
  SWINGIN' GATES
Max Kaminsky (*tpt*); Jack
  Teagarden (*tbn, vcl*); Ernie
  Caceres (*clt*); Norma Tea-
  garden (*p*).

Chinatown, My Chinatown	Commodore FL20015
Big T Blues	—
Rockin' Chair	—
Pitchin' a Bit Short	—

December 12th, 1944
GEORGE WETTLING'S NEW
  YORKERS
Joe Thomas (*tpt*); Jack Tea-
  garden (*tbn, vcl*); Coleman
  Hawkins (*ten*); Hank
  D'Amico (*clt*); Herman
  Chittison (*p*).

You Brought a New Kind of Love	Mercury M625071
Home	—
Somebody Loves Me	—

December 12th, 1944
EDDIE CONDON AND HIS
    ORCHESTRA
Bobby Hackett (*tpt*); Jack Tea-
    garden (*tbn, vcl*); Pee Wee
    Russell (*clt*); Gene Schroeder
    (*p*).

The Sheik of Araby	Decca DL8304, Brunswick (E)LA8577
Somebody Loves Me	Brunswick (E) LA8518

May 17th, 1947
LOUIS ARMSTRONG ALL STARS—
    TOWN HALL CONCERT
Louis Armstrong (*tpt, vcl*);
    Jack Teagarden (*tbn, vcl*);
    Peanuts Hucko (*clt*); Bobby
    Hackett (*tpt*); Sidney Catlett
    (*d*).

Ain't Misbehavin'	Victor LPM1443, HMV (E) DLP1015*	
Rockin' Chair	—	—
Back o' Town Blues	—	—
Pennies from Heaven	—	—
Save It Pretty Mama	—	—
St. James Infirmary	—	—

August 6th, 1947
EDDIE CONDON AND HIS
    ORCHESTRA
Wild Bill Davison (*cnt*); Jack
    Teagarden (*tbn, vcl*); Pee
    Wee Russell (*clt*); Gene
    Schroeder (*p*).

Rose of the Rio Grande	Decca DL8304, Brunswick (E) LA8542
Aunt Hagar's Blues	Decca DL8304, Brunswick (E) LA8542

November 30th, 1947
SATCHMO AT SYMPHONY HALL
Louis Armstrong (*tpt, vcl*); Jack
Teagarden (*tbn, vcl*); Barney
Bigard (*clt*); Dick Cary (*p*);
Arvell Shaw (*bs*); Sidney
Catlett (*d*); Velma Middleton
(*vcl*).

King Porter Stomp	Decca DL8037, Brunswick (E) LAT801/7	
Black and Blue	—	—
Royal Garden Blues	—	—
Lover	—	—
Stars Fell on Alabama	—	—
C Jam Blues	—	—
Baby Won't You Please Come Home	—	—
How High the Moon	—	—
Boff Boff	—	—
I Cried for You	Decca DL8038, Brunswick (E) LAT801/8	
Since I Fell for You	—	—
Tea for Two	—	—
Body and Soul	—	—
Muskrat Ramble	—	—
Steak Face	—	—
On the Sunny Side of the Street	—	—
High Society	—	—
That's My Desire	—	—

April 24th and 26th, 1950
LOUIS ARMSTRONG ALL STARS
(As previous personnel except

Earl Hines (*p*); Cozy Cole (*d*) replaces Cary and Catlett).

That's for Me	Decca DL5280, Brunswick (E) LA8534
Fine and Dandy	— —
Baby Won't You Please Come Home	— —
I Surrender Dear	— —
Russian Lullaby	— —
Panama	Decca DL5279, Brunswick (E) LA8537
New Orleans Function	— —
My Bucket's Got a Hole in It	— —
Bugle Call Rag	— —

January 30th, 1951
SATCHMO AT PASADENA (same personnel as previously).

Indiana	Decca DL8041, Brunswick (E) LAT8019
Baby It's Cold Outside	— —
Way Down Yonder in New Orleans	— —
Stardust	— —
The Hucklebuck	— —
Honeysuckle Rose	— —
My Monday Date	— —
Just You, Just Me	— —
You Can Depend on Me	— —
That's a Plenty	— —

Early 1952
BEN POLLACK AND HIS PICK-A-RIB BOYS
Charlie Teagarden (*tpt*); Jack Teagarden (*tbn*); Matty Matlock (*clt*); Ray Sherman (*p*).

Mighty Like a Rose	Savoy MG15017, London (E) LTZ-C15081

November 4th, 1953
BIG T'S JAZZ
Charlie Teagarden (*tpt*); Jack Teagarden (*tbn, vcl*); Jay St. John (*clt*); Ray Bauduc (*d*).

I Gotta Right to Sing the Blues	Decca DL8304, Brunswick (E) LAT8229
I'm Gonna Stomp Mr. Henry Lee	— —
Body and Soul	— —
Love Me	— —

October 1954
MEET THE NEW JACK TEAGARDEN
Ruby Braff (*tpt*); Jack Teagarden (*tbn, vcl*); Lucky Thompson (*ten*); Ken Kersey (*p*); Milt Hinton (*bs*).

Lover	Urania UJLP1001, UJLP1205
A Hundred Years From Today	— —
St. James Infirmary	— —

October 1954
THE NEW JACK TEAGARDEN PLAYS AND SINGS (as last).

After You've Gone	Urania UJLP1002,* UJLP1205
Blue and Esoteric	— —
Stars Fell on Alabama	— —
Christmas Song	— —

November 1954
JACK TEAGARDEN AND HIS ORCHESTRA
Jimmy McPartland, Dick Cary (*tpt*); Jack Teagarden (*tbn,*

vcl); Ed Hall (*clt*); Jo Jones
or Ray Bauduc (*d*).

Eccentric	Bethlehem BCP32, London (E) LTZ-N150/77*
Original Dixieland One Step	— —
Bad Acting Woman	— —
High Society	— —
Davenport Blues	— —
Music to Love By	— —
Meet Me Where They Play the Blues	— —
King Porter Stomp	— —
Misery and the Blues	— —
Riverboat Shuffle	— —

January 18th, 1955
BIG T'S JAZZ
Johnny Windhurst (*tpt*); Jack
   Teagarden (*tbn, vcl*); Hank
   D'Amico (*clt*); Dick Well-
   stood (*p*).

Persian Rug	Decca DL8304, Brunswick (E) LAT822/9
Love Me or Leave Me	— —
Nobody Knows the Trouble I've Seen	— —
Blue River	— —

October 18th-19th, 1955
BOBBY HACKETT AND HIS JAZZ
   BAND-COAST CONCERT
Bobby Hackett (*tpt*); Jack Tea-
   garden, Abe Lincoln (*tbn*);
   Matty Matlock (*clt*).

Big Butter and Egg Man	Capitol T692, Capitol (E) LC6824
New Orleans	— —
That's a Plenty	— —

Basin Street Blues	Capitol T692, Capitol (E) LC6824
Muskrat Ramble	— —
I Guess I'll Have to Change My Plans	— —
Royal Garden Blues	— —
Struttin' With Some Barbecue	— —
Fidgety Feet	— —

January 1956
THIS IS TEAGARDEN
Charlie Teagarden (*tpt*); Jack Teagarden (*tbn, vcl*); Eddie Miller (*ten*); Ray Sherman (*p*).

Aunt Hagar's Children's Blues	Capitol T721, Cap (E) T721
After You've Gone	— —
The Sheik of Araby	— —
Beale Street Blues	— —
If I Could Be with You	— —
I'm Coming Virginia	— —
Fare Thee Well to Harlem	— —
Stars Fell on Alabama	— —
My Kinda Love	— —
Monday Date	— —
Old Pigeon Toed Joad	— —
Peg o' My Heart	— —

Late 1956
JACK TEAGARDEN—SWING LOW SWEET SPIRITUAL
Jack Teagarden (*tbn, vcl*) with studio orchestra and choir directed by Van Alexander.

Joshua Fit the Battle of Jericho	Capitol T820, Capitol (E) EAP1-820
Nobody Knows the Trouble I've Seen	Capitol T820, Capitol (E) EAP1-820

Gonna Shout All Over God's Heaven	Capitol T820, EAP2-820	Capitol (E)
Swing Low Sweet Chariot	—	—
Sometimes I Feel like a Motherless Child	Capitol T820,	Capitol (E) EAP3-820
This Train	—	—
Shadrack	—	—
Sing and Shout	—	—
Deep River	—	Capitol (E) EAP2-820
Ezekiel Saw the Wheel	—	—
Goin' Home	—	Capitol (E) EAP1-820
Git on Board Little Children	—	—

1957
PAUL WHITEMAN FIFTIETH
    ANNIVERSARY
Large band. Jack Teagarden
    (*tbn*, *vcl*) featured in the
    following numbers:

Jeepers Creepers	Grand Award 33-901
Basin Street Blues	—
Lazy River	—
Christmas Night in Harlem	—
Lover	—

July 4th, 1957
RED ALLEN, KID ORY AND JACK
    TEAGARDEN AT NEWPORT
Henry 'Red' Allen (*tpt*); Jack
    Teagarden, Kid Ory, J. C.
    Higginbotham (*tbn*); Buster
    Bailey (*clt*); Claude Hopkins
    (*p*).

Basin Street Blues	Verve MGV8233, Columbia (E) 33CX1/0106
China Boy	— —

High Society	Verve MGV8233, Columbia (E) 33CX1/0106

July 8th, 1957
BUD FREEMAN'S SUMMA CUM
  LAUDE ORCHESTRA
Billy Butterfield (*tpt*); Jack Teagarden (*tbn*); Bud Freeman (*ten*); Peanuts Hucko (*clt*); George Wettling (*d*).

Prince of Wails	Victor LPM1508
Jack Hits the Road	—
47th and State	—
There'll Be Some Changes Made	—
At the Jazz Band Ball	—
You Took Advantage of Me	Victor LPM1644
I Cover the Waterfront	—

September 1957
JAZZ ULTIMATE
Bobby Hackett (*tpt*); Jack Teagarden (*tbn*, *vcl*); Ernie Caceres (*bar*); Gene Schroeder (*p*).

	Capitol T933,	Capitol (E) T933
Indiana		
Oh, Baby	—	—
It's Wonderful	—	—
I Found a New Baby	—	—
Sunday	—	—
Baby Won't You Please Come Home	—	—
Everybody Loves My Baby	—	—
Mama's Gone, Good-bye	—	—
Way Down Yonder in New Orleans	—	—
55th and Broadway	—	—
's Wonderful	—	—

Early 1958
SHADES OF NIGHT
Jack Teagarden (*tbn*) featured.

Autumn Leaves	Capitol T1143
Diane	—
Alone Together	—
Mixed Emotions	—
While We're Young	—
Street of Tears	—
Someone Else's Love	—
Strange	—
Junk Man	—
Cabin in the Sky	—
Autumn Serenade	—
If Love is Good to Me	—

April 1958
BIG T'S DIXIELAND BAND
Dick Oakley (*tpt*); Jack Teagarden (*tbn, vcl*); Jerry Fuller
   (*clt*); Don Ewell (*p*).

Mobile Blues	Capitol T1095, Capitol (E) T1095	
Wolverine Blues	—	—
Tishomingo Blues	—	—
Someday You'll be Sorry	—	—
Rippa-Tutti	—	—
Dallas Blues	—	—
Casanova's Lament	—	—
Walleritis	—	—
Doctor Jazz	—	—
China Boy	—	—
Weary River	—	—

Index

204

JACK TEAGARDEN